Prosperous Revelations

Prosperous Revelations:
Invest Better, Live Better, Retire Better & Give Better

Madrona Financial Services, LLC
MadronaFinancial.com
2911 Bond St Suite 200
Everett, WA 98201
Phone: (844) MADRONA
Fax: (425) 252-4779

First edition January 2015

ISBN: 978-0-692-32403-5

Edited by Tamela M. Rich

Cover design by Nizam Uddin Shimul

Interior design by Andy Ciordia

DEDICATION

I would like to dedicate this book to all of my friends and supporters at Christ Church Kirkland, and specifically Tong Pineda. I so appreciate the continual support I receive from this amazing group of people and the encouragement to not be afraid to use my gifts to create something new.

Also, my wife Tracie was there for every chapter, asking questions and helping refine my thoughts and my words. She is a believer in excellence and her contribution lies throughout the pages of this book.

~Brian K. Evans

This book is dedicated in memory of my dad, Don Aaron Curtis. Much of what I learned regarding business and finance, the good and the bad, I learned from my dad. May this book be a fitting tribute to the single most impactful man in my life. Love you Dad, Dale Raymond xooxoooo

~Dale Raymond Curtis

TABLE OF CONTENTS

FOREWORD   1

ACKNOWLEDGMENTS   3

INTRODUCTION   5

PART ONE: INVEST BETTER   7
  Basic Diversification   11
  Rules, Rules, Rules   13
  Drinking Your Company's Kool-Aid   17
  False Loyalties   19
  Learn the Forward Price/Earnings Ratio   21
  Add a "G" to the Price/Earnings Ratio   23
  Don't Try to Time the Markets   25
  Follow the Money   29
  Not so Warm and Fuzzy!   31
  The ABCs of Fees   33
  Regular is to Deluxe as Mutual Fund is to ETF   35
  When Up Means Down, and Down Means Up   37
  God Loves and Cares for Imperfect People   39
  My Great Big Math Trophy   41

PART TWO: LIVE BETTER   43
  Tax Tail Wagging the Dog   47
  Proceeds and Cash Flow and Gains, Oh My!   49
  I Want it Now!   51
  Four Flavors of Tax   53
  The Shawshank Redemption, Clarified   55

PART THREE: RETIRE BETTER   57
  Music Lessons   61
  Christmas Morning or Christmas Eve?   65
  Does Congress Hate Old People?   67
  Christians, Mechanics, and Your 401(k)   69
  Making Life Insurance Less Confusing   71

More? Better!   75
I'm Older, Can I Afford to See the Doctor?   77
Insurance Meets Wall Street   79
You Can't Spend Dirt   81

PART FOUR: GIVE BETTER   85
Step On Up   87
Grandma, Please Don't Give Me Your House!   89
How to Ruin Your Grandkids With One Sentence   91
Raoul, The Pool Boy   93
Who Gets the Cactus Plant?   95
Have Your Cake and Eat It Too!   97
When Giving Definitely Feels Good!   99

FOREWORD

When I first met Brian Evans and Dale Curtis over five years ago, it was to bring investment strategies that didn't yet exist, even though there was a viable need within the marketplace. Those investment strategies are now available as exchange-traded funds, which perhaps are better known by their more common acronym of ETF. As someone whose profession and passion is rooted in the ETF industry, the unique fund structure has established itself as a modern technology, much like a smartphone, that champions itself on its accessibility, efficiency and everyday transparency—a very important feature that allows a clearer understanding of what the ETF actually does and contains.

Before we get way too far ahead of ourselves and begin talking about investment strategies and funds—which this book is not about—most items and events that guide us in life begin with a plan. The things that guide us must also begin with everyday transparency so that we can have a clearer understanding of the goals we're setting out to accomplish in life, whether they're financial, educational, professional or personal goals.

A unique and refreshing feature about Brian and Dale's book is that they don't tell you how you must invest or solicit you for business, but rather they clearly articulate how you, the reader, can be guided onto the right course to better evaluate your options and to ask the appropriate, and sometimes difficult, questions. This book provides those seeking a firm footing with their finances and long-term goals a compass and resource to seek counsel and services on your own well-informed terms. The aim here is to enlighten, educate and empower.

I have been working in the finance world for a quarter century and I can undeniably attest that no one individual or firm has it all figured out. Although there are many talented people and successful organizations that do exist and can be tremendous resources, it's important for an individual to figure that out on their own rather than just assume or take someone's word as gospel. Just like with so many aspects of life, investing and financial planning are fluid processes that when we decide to engage with information and seek understanding, we're better off for it.

Remember, there are going to be ups and downs with all facets of financial planning, just as there are in all chapters of this life journey. Mistakes and hardships can happen but that doesn't mean they have to become the main theme or dominate our lives–people can not only learn from their mistakes, but also learn how to thrive from such experiences, and Brian and Dale share some very personal and professional experiences to explain different situations and circumstances. They provide their perspective from years of sharpening their expertise and honing their understanding. It's important to have a plan and their keen, straightforward counsel shows that humor can still exist. Such an undertaking doesn't need to be daunting or seem artificial. Financial planning is not only part of life, but it can even be fun as much as a revelation.

If I may leave you with one piece of advice as you head into reading this book, it is to stay positive and keep moving forward. Matters of tax, investments and estate planning are not prohibitive barriers but rather areas that may leave you, your family and your legacy in a comfortable place. I believe, and hope, Brian and Dale will help make this journey more transparent for you.

- Noah Hamman
Founder & CEO of AdvisorShares Investments, LLC
January 1, 2015

ACKNOWLEDGMENTS

Dr. Sheri Curtis, for your unwavering support of me and my crazy ventures, and for your unconditional love. I love you!

Brian Evans, you are more than a friend and co-author; you're a brother both in this life and the one to come. Thank you for asking me to write with you—this was fun.

Whitney and Dan Kean, and Cayla Curtis, for allowing this dad the freedom to improvise on the fly. You make it easy to be your dad. I will always love each one of you, no matter...

Verlene Curtis and Sharon Thompson, because two moms are always better! You have both loved me when I have been-less-than lovable and that has made a difference in who I am today. I love you both so much.

Dave Locke and Tom Thompson, two more dads and giant men in my life. Dave, for introducing me to investing, and Tom, for showing me that it's good to push against the status quo. I miss and love you both.

Bob Abraham, my first business partner and outside investor. I love you Bob.

~Dale Raymond Curtis

Rebecca McCarthy and Tracie Evans for their contributions to Part Two.

Tamela Rich – This book would have never been written without you and I am grateful for your presence on this project and the expertise you deployed to bring it to fruition.

~Brian K. Evans and Dale Raymond Curtis

INTRODUCTION

Dale and I share the philosophy that you should earn money the way God gifted you to do so, then pay professionals to do what you either can't—or shouldn't—do yourself.

That was a valuable lesson that has served me well in life and certainly has saved me both time and money. It also prevented me from experiencing the consequences of my misguided efforts to re-plumb the bathroom, diagnose my medical ailments, and administer the company's intranet!

Investments, taxes, retirement and legacy planning are also tasks that should be managed while in the confidence of professionals. While there are countless books written on each of these topics, none hit specifically on how they can all be managed simultaneously, in a cohesive way, to help you maximize the potentials benefits of each. There are synergies to gain from addressing these topics in concert, as we do here and in our advisory practice.

Drawing upon over 65 years of our combined professional work experience, Dale and I found that our clients repeatedly ask us the same questions. Since financial questions often arise outside of traditional office hours—when our clients are always welcome to call and speak to us personally—we decided to write *Prosperous Revelations*.

Prosperous Revelations is divided into four Parts, Invest Better, Live Better, Retire Better and Give Better. Each Part has several topical chapters which draw largely upon my anecdotes. I tried lightened up topics that are too often addressed with statistics and legalese. Lighten up, readers!

Dale chimes in occasionally throughout the book, including a personal story that illustrates the consequences of poor financial planning on his parents' part—they were devastating. He vowed when possible, to help others avoid the same experience.

The lessons Dale learned through the impact of his father's financial legacy continues to resonate in his life. Not all of the lessons are bad though, as much of the entrepreneurial spirit that radiates within Dale had its origins in the life of his father, which is why he dedicated his part in this book to him.

Periodically throughout this book, you will see advice or information highlighted in gray. We've developed these suggestions or found this information to be helpful helpful during our extensive practical experience conducting financial planning for our clients and wanted to share them with you, the reader.

Brian K. Evans
November 17, 2014

PART ONE:
INVEST BETTER

Investment management does not have to be complicated to achieve the best results. It starts with your goals, time horizon and risk tolerance and ends with a comprehensive financial plan that mitigates your exposure to risk, minimizes your tax liability and maximizes your potential returns.

Investment Advisors are cliché, a dime a dozen, each thinking that they have "it" all figured out forever. What is "it?"

"It" is how to make money while "never" losing any. Right?

How many ads do you see on a daily basis talking about investing and making money? How many talk about losing money? Exactly, ZERO! Why is this? How do you think investment advisors can get you to invest using their firm if you are already thinking about losing money when you meet them?

What is the average person to do? How do you determine which advisor to use to help grow your investments?

There are some general principles to adhere to when looking for investment advice, or when looking to employ an investment professional or firm.

First, you want to do business with advisors that do not custody assets. "Custody" means that they physically hold your cash, securities, and investments and only certain companies are qualified to do so. Generally speaking, it is best to separate the advisor and their advice from having access to your cash and investments. Assets should be held at a third-party firm that is registered to do so, such as Fidelity Investments or TD Ameritrade. This will help protect you from a potential Bernie Madoff-type situation.[1]

The second principle is to make sure that your professional or their firm has a strategy and a process for investing—and that they follow it. Process takes the emotion out of investing and helps to moderate investment behavior. Many firms will take your money, place it in a few different index funds, and leave it alone while never actively helping you manage your money. You could do this on your own!

---

[1]   If you aren't familiar with this reference, Bernie Madoff ran a multi-million dollar confidence game that defrauded more than 8,000 investors. For more information, read one of these books: *Too Good to Be True* by Erin Arvedlund, *Betrayal* by Andrew Kirtzman or *Madoff with the Money* by Jerry Oppenheimer.

Professionals should have expertise to offer you—expertise that they earned through a lot of hard work and experience. This is what you are paying for and if they don't have it then why pay for it?

Ask yourself, "What am I paying them for? What is their value-add? What are they providing that I can't get anywhere else?"

If they can't provide the answers to those questions for you, if they can't articulate what makes them unique and specifically, what their uniqueness will do for you, then you should run away and run fast! You could do this on your own—but you shouldn't. Find the right people to work with and pay them; you will be glad that you did.

The third principle is transparency—transparency from your advisor and transparency with the investments they are choosing for you. This is an integrity issue. An advisor and their company must disclose fees, commissions (there may not be any), conflicts of interests, company policies and procedures, prudence, whether they custody assets, and so on. They are going to become your financial partner and similar to marriage, you should not enter into the arrangement without full disclosure.

Taking my marriage analogy a bit further, get to know them; court them for a while; have multiple meetings before you decide to give them your life savings to invest. Don't rush to place your trust in them. Start to build trust through the interview process as you look to learn more about their business practices, investment process, and company personnel and policies.

Finally, back to losing money. Be sure to ask them when they lost money—it should be "top of mind" for them and something that is easy to report to you. Why? Because we all have lost money. In our business we aspire to not lose money but we remember very clearly when we have. In similar fashion to a doctor who takes an oath to do no harm but sometimes does some harm, honest financial advisors, looking out for your best interests, will strive to do their best while being clear about when they fell short.

We seek to minimize losses by using instruments that take emotion out of the investment process. Mutual funds and ETFs do just that and they allow us to draw upon the expertise of actively-managed fund managers. As a matter of fact, we make extensive use of "funds of funds" and "ETFs of ETFs."

We are not stock pickers and this book is not designed to help readers pick stocks or time the markets.

Investors must sign an advisory agreement before they engage a financial advisor and move assets into the advisor's control. The agreements are governed by the Securities and Exchange Commission and must disclose several things, including:

- Services to be provided
- Duration of the contract
- Advisory fee and the formula for computing the fee
- Amount of the prepaid fee to be returned in case of contract termination or nonperformance

Advisory agreements can cover a range of subjects. Ours advises clients who hold individual stocks in self-directed 401(k)s to roll them over into an ETF or mutual fund. Occasionally clients wish to exclude from our management stocks that they are "sentimentally attached to," for example, one that they inherited from a family member. While we will agree to such an exclusion, after reading the chapter "False Loyalties" you might think twice about getting sentimental about any financial instrument.

We encourage investors to read and discuss the advisory agreements in detail. Better not to enter into a relationship with an advisor whose philosophy differs from yours than to be faced with unwinding that relationship later.

Bring together a team of three experts: CPA, Financial Advisor (RIA), and an Estate Planning Attorney (EPA). Put them in the same room and make them work together for your benefit. Give them complete authorization to disclose information to one another on a real-time basis. They should all know what you have, where it's located, how it's being used, how it's held, and where it's going when you die.

Typically, you can get to the other two through the one relationship that you may have. For instance, if you have a CPA, ask for referrals to an RIA and EPA.

Basic Diversification

One of my more interesting diversification stories happened in 1999, right before the dot-com crash. I was meeting with a prospective client but I think he was more interested in bragging about his portfolio's results in 1999 than in hiring a financial advisor.

I asked him if his portfolio was diversified, and he responded with an emphatic *"yes."* He went on to say that he held Microsoft, Intel, Dell, Cisco and Hewlett-Packard. Obviously this type of so-called "diversification" did little to help when the technology sector crashed the following year.

The goal of diversification is for the value of assets not to move in the same direction all the time.

Here is a more alarming true story of an attorney who called me to counsel her 82-year-old client. The widow had a $2.5 million estate.

I proceeded to explain my views on asset allocation, talking about stocks, bonds, commodities, and broad market funds with hundreds of different positions each, etc. She volleyed back, "I have no interest in your risky stock market investments. I'm a conservative investor!"

I then explained the concept of "all your eggs in one basket," and she retorted that her investment was exempt from my concern. According to the client, her investment could never fluctuate and was as safe as a bank CD. The air was tense so we agreed to disagree and I left the meeting.

Our original meeting took place in June of 2008. Three months later, her $2.5 million of Washington Mutual stock was completely worthless, and she was bankrupt. I have to admit that I thought Washington Mutual was a buy when I chatted with her. I remember suggesting at least selling some of it. But no matter how much I may like a particular investment, I also know you need to have multiple baskets, since there are no sure things!

Rules, Rules, Rules

I know! I don't like rules either so let's call this financial principle, "The Proposition of 100." This suggestion is the starting point for building a conservative retirement portfolio that mitigates risk and creates a safe haven for a portion of your assets.

Ideally, as we age, our investment portfolios should move from a position of greater risk to one that includes less risk exposure. One methodology that successful planners employ to achieve this goal is to start with the number 100 and subtract your age (for couples, use the average of the two ages). The result is the maximum percentage of market risk (potential for investment loss due to factors that affect overall financial markets) you should undertake in your portfolio.

Here is an example: A 50-year-old with a $500,000 portfolio: 100-50=50%. 50% or $250,000 is the maximum suggested amount to be placed at risk in the market.

Sample Conservative Model*

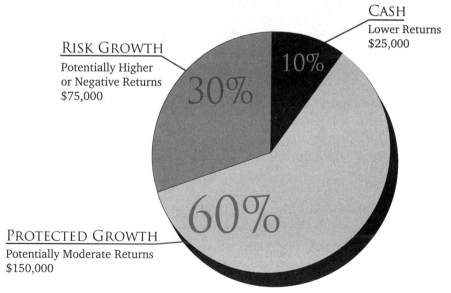

CASH
Lower Returns
$25,000

RISK GROWTH
Potentially Higher
or Negative Returns
$75,000

10%

30%

60%

PROTECTED GROWTH
Potentially Moderate Returns
$150,000

*Investing $250,000 in the market.

What do you do with the money you have not invested in the market? Determine how much cash you need and set aside the appropriate percentage for that purpose. Here's a simple approach:

Liquid cash = (MB x Months) + STP

MB	Monthly Budget
MONTHS	Number of months you want to have liquid cash available
STP	Short-term purchases not accounted for in your monthly budget (furniture, appliances, cars, home improvements, vacations) over the same number of months (Months)

Finally, this leaves a remainder to be placed inside a safe money asset such as a fixed-index annuity (FIA) that can also have an income rider[2] with it to provide future income that you can never outlive.

FIXED-INDEX ANNUITIES - PROTECTED

An Indexed Annuity's interest rate is tied to an index such as the S&P 500. If the index goes up, the owner of the annuity is credited with a portion of the increase in the index and those gains are retained in the contract. If the index goes down, both the principal and previous years' gains are retained, and the owner of the annuity loses no ground.

Using the example above with a balance of $250,000, I decide to place $50,000 (10% of portfolio) into cash equivalents and $200,000 (40% of portfolio) into principal-protected assets.[3] FIAs on average yield[4] better than CD rates. While both have a surrender term, the yield makes FIAs better.

Constructing a portfolio with market risk assets, cash equivalents, and fixed-index annuities decreases risk and lessens the probability of overwhelming financial setbacks.

---

2   Investopedia defines "rider" as provision of an insurance policy that is purchased separately from the basic policy and that provides additional benefits at additional cost. Standard policies usually leave little room for modification or customization, beyond choosing deductibles and coverage amounts. Riders help policyholders create insurance products that meet their specific needs.

3   Examples of principal-protected assets are FIAs, CDs, fixed-annuities, and money-market accounts. In general, assets that don't go down in value.

4   According to Investopedia, "yield" is the income return on an investment. This refers to the interest or dividends received from a security and is usually expressed annually as a percentage based on the investment's cost, its current market value or its face value.

Anyone who endured the stock market crash of 2008 understands the vulnerability that comes with being "all in." Investors lacking the type of assets in their portfolios that could "not go down" were hit hard—losses averaging 30%.

Those with longer time horizons, years to recoup their losses, were shocked but not dismayed—time was on their side. But what about the people who were within five years of retiring? What was the impact of this crash on them and their families? Some sacrificed good health while the dreams of others and the retirements of most were shattered due in large part to the misallocation of assets.

While striving to accumulate wealth, investors place capital at risk in exchange for potential growth but as retirement approaches their objective must shift to risk reduction for the sake of asset preservation. The longer you have to prepare for retirement, generally, the more risk you are willing to bear with your investments. But as you look to step back from the workforce, you become less tolerant of investment losses, both practically and emotionally. No one wants to see, nor can many withstand, hard-earned retirement money lost just before it needs to be deployed. This dictates a strategy that is necessary to preserve assets for retirement, one that mitigates risk and is not 'all in'

The Proposition of 100 is better than a suggestion, it is a sound approach to portfolio and retirement planning. It is a rule.

FIA VALUES CLIMB OVER TIME—EVEN WHEN MARKETS ARE DOWN

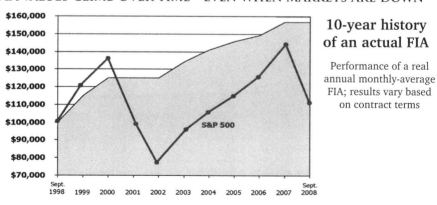

10-year history of an actual FIA

Performance of a real annual monthly-average FIA; results vary based on contract terms

Source: Coalition for Fixed Products

DRINKING YOUR COMPANY'S KOOL-AID

As an employer, I appreciate working with employees who truly believe in our company and its mission to help people. If you are an employee, no matter how much you may love your company, you still need to realize that sometimes bad things happen to good companies.

Let's take, for example, the thousands of Enron employees who, in 2001, went from working for a high-flyer to the unemployment line. This is not to say that Enron was a "good" company; it was really a complex farce of a company. Very few people knew it at the time. The poor workers were unaware of the internal problems. When the underlying deception was discovered, most of the workers lost their 401(k) retirement accounts, too.

The loss of these accounts wasn't actually due directly to Enron's collapse. The loss was due to employees who "drank the Kool-Aid" and put their entire retirement nest egg into one place—Enron stock. Many employees had six-figure jobs with seven-figure 401(k)s, most of which were invested in company stock. Therefore, when Enron collapsed, employees lost not only their jobs, but also their nest eggs.

In another example, consider the stock boy who came to me for investment advice. He was no ordinary stock boy; he was one of the first employees of Amazon.com. When I met with him, he had $1.5 million of exercisable stock options. I suggested he cash in and profit from his fortune.

He proceeded to tell me that I was basically an idiot because Amazon was the greatest company ever. Knowledge of his two small children, tiny apartment, $13-an-hour job, and pregnant wife prompted me to overcome my pride. The year was 1999, and the technology part of the stock market was rising dramatically. I thought Amazon was a good investment, but in the case of expiring stock options, timing is a bigger issue.

Since he would not take my advice, I suggested he sell half of his options and invest the rest into a residence for his growing family. He went to tell me off as an ignorant so-and-so. I have no idea why he wanted to meet with an advisor in the first place, other than to gloat about his good fortune.

Six months later, the stock market crashed. Six months later, his stock option strike price was higher than the value of the stock, meaning his options were completely worthless, and they expired with no value. No house, no investments, but he still had his $13-an-hour job!

False Loyalties

We all treasure the quality of loyalty. Sometimes it is important to define what or who we are being loyal to.

For instance, I have had many clients in the Seattle area explain to me what Microsoft has done for their life and finances. With that in mind, they tell me to never sell the stock due to their emotional commitment. Others have inherited stock from a loved one and they want to cling to that possession like they would to Grandma's old wedding ring or Grandpa's collection of family photographs.

Very often, we investors tie our decisions to emotional considerations. Stocks are traded on what's called the secondary market. For example, if I purchase 1,000 shares of Microsoft, none of the money goes to Bill Gates or to Microsoft. Instead, it goes to the seller of that stock who could be Mrs. Neusbaum from Atlanta. When I sell Microsoft, it may be to a buyer that day named Fred from Walla Walla. Microsoft and Bill Gates have nothing to do with these transactions, since these trades are on the secondary markets. Microsoft received its money during the early eighties during their initial public offering (IPO).

Personally, I am inspired by Bill Gates, and I admire his company. And I absolutely adore his company when it is trading at $25 per share. I like Microsoft as an investment at $40 per share. I want nothing to do with Microsoft at $200 per share.[5] So my like or dislike of a company stock can be completely based on the current price, not on the company itself.

Based on Market Price	Price/Earnings	PEG*
One Year Ago (6/30/13)	13.8x	0.8x
Current (6/30/14)	15.6x	1.5x
25-Year Average	15.5x	1.4x

* "PEG" will be defined in a later section

It's interesting to note that most of us spend countless hours shopping for the very best deal on most everything we buy. When we search for real estate, for example, we look at several houses and ask our real estate agents for "comps" on comparable houses to be sure we buy at the right price. For some reason investors don't bring this mentality into

---

5   Of course this assumes that the current management team and business strategy are unchanged.

choosing their investments. Many of them fall in love with a certain company and hold on, no matter what is happening in the market or what the stock's price has become.

I also run into a similar issue when discussing the notion of investing with the goal of social responsibility. Many people believe that when they buy stocks on the secondary stock exchanges, they are making a big difference in the world. It's a nice thought, but not exactly true. My advice would be to invest in a valuation-centric and diversified way. When it comes to philanthropy, give your time, money or support directly to the causes of your choice, not through the stock markets.

LEARN THE FORWARD PRICE/EARNINGS RATIO

The Forward Price/Earnings Ratio, or Forward PE Ratio[6] is the second-most important measure of the value of a company or of a market sector. You may never know this from watching business shows on TV as they focus on hundreds of esoteric details in trying to predict the direction of a stock.

It drives me crazy when the business announcer on the radio says, "The markets are up today due to good pork belly futures price reports coming out of Thailand." This is gibberish, in my opinion. Most of what the broadcast media says about short-term movements of the markets is a bunch of hooey.

Remember, when we invest in stock, we usually aren't giving any of our investment directly to the company, since stocks trade on the secondary markets. Investors purchase stocks because they believe the company will earn a lot of profit in the future, relative to what they are paying for that stock. The goal is to buy stocks when we think they are undervalued. This is why I adore Microsoft at $25, like it at $40 and want nothing to do with it at $200.

The "forward" of the PE Ratio is the expectation of next year's profit per share based on the average estimate from all analysts covering that company. For example, if Amazon trades at $90 per share, and projected earnings per share next year are $6, then 90/6 yields a Forward PE ratio of 15. The long term historical average PE ratio of the U.S. stock market is about 16 times earnings. The lower the PE Ratio, the better.

You are paying 15 times net profit to own Amazon at $90 with expected earnings of $6 over the coming year. How accurate are these estimates you ask? To answer that question, think about all the times you hear about a company beating analyst estimates, or falling short by 1 or 2 cents per share.

So how can this help? In my other book, *The Black Book on Personal Finance*[tm], I performed a case study on the stock market crash in the early 2000's. What I concluded was that we did not have a market crash. In-

---

6   Defined by Investopedia as a valuation ratio of a company's current share price compared to its per-share earnings. Calculated as: Market Value per Share / Earnings per Share (EPS)

stead, we had a crash of the part of the market that had an average PE of 200 times earnings (NASDAQ).

The rest of the market did just fine during this time, and the sectors with single digit PEs had huge rallies! So investors who applied this one principal could have made money during the dot-com market crash. Investing based on PE is a way to apply the concept of "buying low." Warren Buffett has made a pretty decent living applying this concept.

ADD A "G" TO THE PRICE/ EARNINGS RATIO

What could be even more predictive than the PE Ratio? The five-year Forward PEG Ratio. This takes the Forward PE we just learned about, and divides it by the 5-year expected growth of the earnings of the company. G stands for growth.

For example, remember that Amazon had a PE of 15. But how does that compare to XYZ utility company with a PE of only 12? XYZ would be a better buy, right? Not necessarily.

Assume that Amazon was projected to grow their earnings by 15% per year over the next five years. Also assume XYZ had a 6% growth of earnings projected. Amazon would have a PEG of 1.00 and XYZ a PEG of 1.50. Lower is better, so even though both companies look good, Amazon looks better. What the PEG is telling me here is for every $100 I invest into Amazon stock, my expected share of company earnings over just the next 5 years should be about $60. This amount calculates to about $50 for XYZ.

How strongly do I feel that the PEG Ratio is the single most important and all-encompassing analytical tool in stock market valuation? Along with some very talented em-

A quick story on how these funds came about. I had never even had the thought of creating my own funds. Then one morning I woke up and my head was completely full of formulas, graphs, methodologies, marketing, and rates of return. It was so full, it literally took over an hour for me to explain all of it to my wife that morning.

While she is not a financial professional she is pretty sharp and well-educated. Although she has wisely discouraged some of my business ideas, I'm grateful that she encouraged me to pursue the project of bringing a new fund to market that would use the PEG ratio.

As I researched what would be involved, I was told over and over by industry analysts that I didn't have enough money, contacts, or clout to even consider a successful launch. They proclaimed the project dead on arrival.

Not so! We launched a fund in June of 2011 on the New York Stock Exchange. In honor of the fund's launching, I was given the privilege of ringing the opening bell on the NYSE.

ployees and the people at AdvisorShares, we were able to spearhead the effort to bring this solution to the public in the form of a Domestic-based Fund and an Internationally-based Fund.[7]

7   Their New York Stock Exchange symbols are FWDD and FWDI, under the Madrona Funds name with Brian Evans, CPA/PFS, Robert Bauer, CPA and Kristi Henderson, CPA/PFS as the lead portfolio managers.

24 MadronaFinancial.com

Don't Try to Time the Markets

I have heard from and seen literally hundreds of stock pickers who claim they have discovered the secret formula to time the markets. Generally they are just playing to people's fears, or their greed. I have yet to read a study where market timing works consistently.

Think about it: if someone can't even predict what the markets will do tomorrow, how can anyone predict what the markets will do in a month, or in a year?

This is a summary of a conversation I had with several clients in early 2009. "Hank" calls to tell me he wants out of the market. I respond that it's his money, and he can do what he feels is best, but I asked Hank a few questions.

Me: Hank, do you think the markets will recover?

Hank: Absolutely.

Me: Do you plan on getting back into the markets?

Hank: Yes.

Me: Okay Hank, when do you plan on doing that?

Hank: When the markets are better!

Me: Okay, define better for me.

Hank: When they are up!

Me: Define "up"...15%? 20%?

Hank: 20%.

Me: Hank, you want out of the markets now and believe they will come back up. So your plan, if successfully executed, has you out of the markets during their recovery, only to re-enter the markets after the recovery. As a result, you will avoid receiving any of the benefit of the 20% gain you believe will happen.

Sheepishly, Hank agrees that plan is doomed for failure.

So what can we do? I suggest targeted asset allocation. Buy low, sell high based on the PEG Ratio. Watch for bubbles and investing fads such as dot-coms and gold when they are too high. Rotate out of bond sectors, or especially out of longer duration bonds when interest rates are rising. In other words, apply good sense to your decision making process and don't just blindly follow the next investment guru.

Targeted asset allocation is the intelligent cousin of market timing. In October of 2011, I knew of this company claiming to have all the answers on market timing. When the Dow hit 12,000, this same company told all their advisors to get out completely and get back in when the Dow hit 9,000.

They said 9,000 was a certainty, not a guess.

Right after this prediction the markets went on a huge multi-year rally with the Dow reaching 16,000. Now what does the market timer do? Stay out forever? Buy after the rally when markets are higher?

Imagine how the advisors would have explained their actions to clients who made no gains during this huge rally, and seemingly had no opportune time to get back into the market.

THE RETIREMENT CHASSIS

I can't tell you how many times I've been told by someone that they went to the bank and bought an IRA. When I asked them what they invested it in, they looked at me funny, and repeated to me slowly that they invested in an IRA—as if they were buying a loaf of bread and that I'm a little slow not to know what an IRA would be.

Retirement accounts come with many names, differing rules and contribution limits, but in the final analysis, they have a lot in common with one another. They generally are pre-tax contributions allowed to grow tax-deferred, only to be taxed as they are distributed to the owner or their beneficiaries.

As we contribute to retirement plans during our working years we can deduct the contributions at the highest marginal tax brackets of our lives. When we start taking distributions from them in retirement, we are generally in a lower tax bracket.

The names of retirement accounts include IRA, 401(k), SEP, SIMPLE, 403(b), 457, Rollover IRA, profit-sharing plan, etc. Generally, upon retirement or separation from your employer, all of these accounts can be rolled into your IRA.

Most of my clients ultimately consolidate all of their plans into their IRA, essentially bundling their accounts. This gives them a clear plan for their future. While employed they could continue to contribute to their current plan at their place of employment and get any company match while allowing their bundle to continue growing according to the plan they've devised with their advisor, using perhaps a Roth IRA.[8]

Retirement accounts are vehicles we use to spread cash flow over our lifetimes. They also serve to spread our tax burden into years with lower tax rates. Managing the many nuances of these plans can have a significant effect on your financial life.

---

8   A Roth IRA is similar to a traditional IRA in that it is a type of individual retirement account. However, contributions are not tax-deductible and qualified withdrawals are tax-free. The account also grows tax-free.

FOLLOW THE MONEY

It can be so frustrating for someone to know where to go for financial advice. Have you ever felt like the professionals you talk to don't really have your best interests at heart? When getting advice, always ask, or at least consider how that person gets paid before taking their advice.

So let's say you decide you need help investing your money.

Say the first person you speak to is your stockbroker. He tells you that stocks and bonds are always the best place to invest and shows you their 75-year average annual return. Then you remember the two recent bear markets and decide to get a second opinion.

When you ask a real estate agent, she will say that you need to buy a rental property because real estate is always a great long-term investment. She will show you her own 50-year average annual returns. But then you remember what happened to the real estate market in 2008, and you remember how many of your friends are underwater on their mortgages today, so you keep searching for better advice.

Then you meet with the insurance agent, who assures you that the long-term safety of a variable annuity is what you need. Funny, you don't remember even sharing much information about your finances with the agent, yet he seems to think he knows exactly what you need. You also remember reading somewhere that the internal fees in variable annuities can be very high, which makes it difficult to achieve your goals. You keep searching.

Next, you go to your banker. She says the

WHAT ARE THE HIGHEST INTEREST RATES YOU REMEMBER RECEIVING ON BANK ASSETS?

	January		January
2002	3.36%	1980	11.47%
2003	1.69%	1981	13.38%
2004	1.13%	1982	15.60%
2005	1.69%	1983	11.84%
2006	3.67%	1984	9.16%
2007	5.22%	1985	10.26%
2008	5.15%	1986	8.02%
2009	2.73%	1987	6.36%
2010	.49%	1988	6.95%
2011	.32%	1989	7.92%
2012	.31%	1990	9.00%

Source: MoneyCafe.com 2012

safest place to invest will be a CD. This sounds reasonable since this is a sure thing. After looking at the current rates, you conclude that there are actually two sure things; you won't lose any principal, *and* you are sure not to beat inflation!

Finally, you go see your most trusted advisor, your CPA. After listening to your ordeal, the CPA agrees that none of these options seem like a good place for the bulk of your investments. You are feeling better now that he confirmed your thoughts, so you ask him what does he recommend? He replies that he doesn't recommend anything. He isn't licensed[9] to give specific investment advice!

You might feel frustrated at this point and ask your CPA why every one of those "financial professionals" had a different suggestion. Aren't they supposed to give you the best advice? The answer is that, by law, they are not required to give you the best advice, since stockbrokers, real estate agents, insurance agents and bankers are not Fiduciary Licensed! They each recommended the instruments that they were licensed to sell, often based on the most attractive commission to them.

Let's face it: If someone is selling widgets, everyone they look at needs a widget.

---

9   Investopedia defines "Fiduciary" as a person legally appointed and authorized to hold assets in trust for another person. The fiduciary manages the assets for the benefit of the other person rather than for his or her own profit.

Not so Warm and Fuzzy!

Most people do not know there are two different licenses for people giving financial advice. One side of the street is the Broker-Dealer, and the other is the Registered Investment Advisor.

How can you tell the difference? If the company the advisor works for has naming rights to a professional football stadium, has offices in every other strip mall, or has an advertising budget bigger than the gross domestic product of Portugal, then they are probably a broker-dealer. But does this matter? I will let you decide after you read the following disclosure required from these firms:

The disclosure for broker-dealers:

> "Your account is a brokerage account and not an advisory account. Our interests may not always be the same as yours. Please ask us questions to make sure you understand your rights and our obligations to you, including the extent of our obligations to disclose conflicts of interest and to act in your best interest. We are paid both by you and, sometimes, by people who compensate us based on what you buy. Therefore, our profits, and our salespersons' compensation, may vary by product and over time."

Not feeling very warm and fuzzy? I don't blame you. I'm not saying any of these people won't care about your best interests, but their requirement is what it is.

Registered Investment Advisors, on the other hand, are a fiduciary of their clients. What does it really mean to be a fiduciary? According to *The Investment Adviser Association's Standards of Practice*:

> "As a fiduciary, an investment advisor has an affirmative duty of care, loyalty, honesty and good faith to act in the best interests of its clients."

The Investment Adviser Association goes on to define what these fiduciary duties are as they relate to the advisory relationship. These generally include the duty to:

- At all times place the interests of clients first;

- Have a reasonable basis for investment advice;

- Seek best execution for clients' securities transactions where the advisor directs such transactions;

- Make investment decisions consistent with any mutually agreed upon client objectives, strategies, policies, guidelines and restrictions;

- Treat clients fairly;

- Make full and fair disclosure to clients of all material facts about the advisory relationship, particularly regarding conflicts of interest; and

- Respect the confidentiality of client information.

Feeling warmer? And yes, the authors of this book are fiduciary licensed registered investment advisor representatives. Bet you didn't see that coming!

THE ABCS OF FEES

Let's say a person just retired and consolidates her entire $1 million portfolio with a financial advisor. The advisor explains to her how a diversified portfolio of mutual funds is what she needs. She is invested on a Tuesday, and at market close the next day, she goes on-line to check her account. Even though there was no change in the market value that day, she sees that she has lost $57,000!

She quickly makes a trip to the advisor to figure out how this mistake happened. There was no mistake, the advisor explains, the mutual funds purchased were front-end load A class shares. She asks him, "Where did all that money go?" Then she answers her own question when she looks out in the parking lot and notices her advisor's new Tesla with the license plate "A-SHARE."

When you invest in a mutual fund, the fund will have five letters for symbols. Pay attention to the fourth letter. This is the one that tells you which fee schedule you will be charged. If the fourth letter is A, you may be paying a sales commission of over 5%, called a front-end load. A-class shares generally have lower annual fees than B- or C-class shares.

A "B" means you will be paying the sales fee when you sell, called a back-end load. This may seem like a good idea when you buy the fund, but I see one major problem here that becomes important when you are thinking of selling, or changing your investment strategy: rather than make a proper decision, many people may hold off selling the funds due to the pain of paying a fee.

C shares are called no load funds, but there is a catch here. Every mutual fund and ETF has an internal charge at differing percentages. Although those C shares do not have a sales fee, they have the highest internal fee of any share class.

To receive the lowest fees, you would look for I or Y shares. These are insitutional class or investor class shares. For most investors however, you have to have millions in that particular fund to qualify for this class. So how does a regular investor navigate this web of higher fee structures?

A financial advisor who is an RIA should be able to help. They cannot receive the loads or sales commissions because this is a conflict of interest. So instead of buying the C shares, they often buy the A shares with the load waived, and still get the lower internal fee.

This would have saved our friend $57,000. More successful RIAs may have enough invested in a fund to qualify for the investor class. In this case you are receiving the lowest possible internal fees on a no load platform.

Regular is to Deluxe as Mutual Fund is to ETF

ETFs are a better investment tool (as detailed below) but sometimes the tool is not available and you have to resort to using mutual funds.

That being said, sometimes you may want a certain mutual fund because you want access to the fund manager. The manager may have a great track record that you have bought into and want to utilize. If this is your goal, be careful. Generally it is better to focus on the process of the fund manager, and other strategies, rather than the managers themselves.

Just when many people have started to understand what a mutual fund[10] is, along comes something new. That something new is the Exchange-Traded Fund or ETF.[11]

ETFs are the fastest growing of all the investment tools. If you are working with an advisor who is compensated solely on sales loads, you may not be aware of them, since there are no sales fees, or multiple classes with ETFs.

Following are some of the advantages ETFs generally have over mutual funds.

- Lower internal fees. ETFs don't have to share internal fees with large trading outfits like mutual funds do, so typically they have lower internal fees. Also, as I just mentioned, only one type of share class is produced per fund, and it has no load.

- Better income tax treatment. Have you ever been told by your CPA that you owe capital gains tax on a mutual fund

---

10   According to Investopedia, a mutual fund is an investment vehicle that is made up of a pool of funds collected from many investors for the purpose of investing in securities such as stocks, bonds, money market instruments and similar assets. Mutual funds are operated by money managers, who invest the fund's capital and attempt to produce capital gains and income for the fund's investors. A mutual fund's portfolio is structured and maintained to match the investment objectives stated in its prospectus.

11   Investopedia defines ETF as a security that tracks an index, a commodity or a basket of assets like an index fund, but trades like a stock on an exchange. ETFs experience price changes throughout the day as they are bought and sold.

you didn't even sell? Most investors have been told this unhappy news. When you invest in a mutual fund, you often purchase the gains from the person who owned the mutual fund before you.. This is usually not the case with ETFs. Also, as you hold a mutual fund over the years, you may be paying taxes on year-end capital gain distributions year after year. This can create a very complex tax recordkeeping situation.

- Intraday trading. If you want to sell your mutual fund at 9:00 a.m. one day, you cannot. They only trade once at the end of a day. ETFs can trade at any time during the day.

- No short-term redemption fees. Many mutual funds charge a 2% penalty on funds sold in the first 90 days after purchase; ETFs do not have this provision.

My final point is that most ETFs are "passive" broad-market indexed based funds. They are meant to approximate the returns of the index they track. These index funds often have a very low annual internal fee because often a computer is selecting the investments based on the size of the underlying holdings in the index.

A new brand of ETF has emerged, called the "actively-managed ETF."[12] These are designed to employ active management and decision-making along with the advantageous ETF structure. The goal of actively-managed ETFs is to combine the inherent advantages over mutual funds, combined with an active approach designed to outperform the typical passive or index methodology.

---

12   Investopedia defines them as an exchange-traded fund that has a manager or team making decisions on the underlying portfolio allocation or otherwise not following a passive investment strategy. An actively managed ETF will have a benchmark index, but managers may change sector allocations, market-time trades or deviate from the index as they see fit. This produces investment returns that will not perfectly mirror the underlying index.

WHEN UP MEANS DOWN, AND DOWN MEANS UP

The bond market can be a little confusing, so I'd like to shed some light on what it is and how it works.

Why is the bond market important? The answer to this question is that there is more money invested in bonds than there is in all of the companies on the New York Stock Exchange combined!

So what is a bond? A bond is a promise. Basically, when you invest in a bond, you are lending money to a government, corporation, municipality, etc., which in turn makes a promise to repay you with interest.

Why don't these entities just borrow money from the bank instead? Bond issuers know they can get a much better interest rate and longer repayment terms by going to investors rather than to banks.

Bond values fluctuate just as often as the stock market fluctuates. Interest rates are in a constant state of change. So when you own a long-term bond (maturity date greater than 10 years) and interest rates increase, the value of your bond decreases, and vice versa. Let me explain.

Let's say you buy a $100,000 20-year bond with a promise to pay you 4% per year. If you hold the bond for 20 years and the entity is able to repay you, you will obviously receive your $100,000 with interest. But most investors do not hold their bonds full term.

So let's say you instead wanted to sell your bond one year after its purchase, but at that time, interest rates on new bonds were 6%. Interest rates have increased, but when you try to sell your bond yielding $2,000 less in interest per year, you won't find a buyer. So, now you have to sell your bond at a discount. You will not even receive $80,000 for this bond on the open market!

This works in reverse too. Had you locked in 6% last year, and interest rates on similar bonds dropped to 4%, you could sell your bond at a premium. Interest rate decreases help bond holders and interest rate increases hurt bond holders.

By looking at the attached graphs, you may make a couple of conclusions. First, bonds can be just as volatile as stocks. Second, we recently hit the 50+ year high (low interest rate) in the bond markets. Interest rates have a likelihood of increasing, lowering bond values.

We may be in what I would term a bond bubble. There are many other factors to consider when buying bonds, but interest rate risk is a primary factor.

GOD LOVES AND CARES FOR IMPERFECT PEOPLE

While I believe God Loves and Cares For Imperfect People, the first letters of this affirmation are also an important acronym (GLCFIP) that helps investors make sure they are covering all of their bases in financial planning.

G: Growth of assets. Every advisor must have a client perform a financial risk tolerance survey for compliance purposes. Once you have done a proper assessment of your personal risk tolerance, there will likely be a percentage of your assets that you wish to allocate to growth. Typical assets in the "growth" category are stocks, real estate and variable annuities. Often this is somewhat determined by your age. A 25-year-old investing in his company 401(k) is likely to put more in growth type assets (typically stock market) than would a 75-year-old.

L: Liquidity. Everybody needs to have some level of liquidity. Loss of job, new roof, unexpected car repair, trip to Europe, regular monthly expenses, these all require cash type liquidity.

Typical liquid assets include checking and savings accounts, stock and bonds, but not bank CDs, due to their early withdrawal penalties. Stocks and bonds are considered liquid if they are not held in retirement accounts. They are not as liquid as cash, but easily converted to cash in about a week if you need it.

Another form of liquidity is the unused line of credit. For those needing quick cash, these can be used immediately, where plans to pay them off can be made shortly thereafter.

CF: Cash Flow. Some people have assets, but very little in cash flow. For example, there was a couple that had very little to spend on a monthly basis. The husband died and the wife was left with a poorly maintained house and lots of money worries. She came to me, and imagine how easy my planning for her became upon finding out her husband had amassed over $15 million in raw land!

Problem was, until she sold something, she still couldn't afford Christmas presents for the grandkids. A balance between growth assets and cash flow needed to be struck. Investors can generally find cash flow using company pensions, annuities with guaranteed lifetime cash flow, paid-off rental properties and Social Security.

I: Inflation. I am barely over 50 years old, but I can still remember 10-cent candy bars and soda pop. I also remember my parents new four-bedroom house on two acres purchased for a whopping $39,000 in 1972. I remember candy cigarettes, flopping around in the open bed of pickup trucks with my brothers, and crossing Interstate 5 on my bicycle, but that's another story.

People are living longer now. When Social Security was created, the average life expectancy was only about 67. Today, for a couple age 62, there is about a one in two chance that one of them will live to be 92. That's 30 years! Inflation must be accounted for in today's retirement planning.

People often neglect to consider spending inflation when planning for retirement. It's critical that you do so. When my dad retired from teaching school nearly 30 years ago, $18,000 annually for life seemed like a fortune. But since there were no cost of living increases in his pension he had to get a part-time job in his later years to keep his standard of living.

P: Protection. Protected assets generally include cash accounts, Bank CDs, fixed annuities, and fixed-index annuities (both with caps and uncapped). Protection is another cyclical topic. I remember when I was 13 years old and I didn't want to take any risk with my hard-earned berry picking money (I still remember earning 12% in my bank savings account). Then I became an entrepreneur and I couldn't even spell the word risk. Now that I'm consulting with so many retirement-age people, protection of principal is really their strongest desire.

Who wants to take the risk of being forced to take a job in their 70's due to investment mistakes in their 60's? Unfortunately, many people suffered great financial misfortune in the two market crashes over the last 15 years. Protection of principal is a paramount financial objective for pre- or post-retirement individuals.

MY GREAT BIG
MATH TROPHY

When I was young, I had a major dilemma. I could not decide if I was going to be a professional football, basketball, or baseball player. This was even before the two-sport stars like Deion Sanders and Bo Jackson proved you could play two professional sports. As the years went by, I earned many trophies such as Gentleman Athlete and the 110% club. It was years later before I learned that these awards were given to the athletes who tried the hardest but really weren't stars.

I did have moderate success in high school athletics, but upon my graduation I realized something very telling to my life. After thousands of hours focused on my athletic endeavors, my grandest trophy of them all, the trophy standing three feet tall was, wait for it, Senior Class Outstanding Math Student. What a rally killer.

I realized that my path and God-given talents were not in the athletic realm, but instead in the world of numbers. Over the years I have discovered that numbers can be a great communication tool, even better than words, which brings us to our next topic. How to define your risk tolerance?

Investment advisors are generally required to ask you for your risk tolerance. Are you conservative, moderate, moderately aggressive, or aggressive? Over the years I have learned that people don't understand these words, and people are aggressive when the markets do well, and they are scared senseless when they are down. I want a new model to discover risk tolerance, so let's get back to my first language: numbers.

Based on prior chapters in this book, let's assume an investor placed 5% of their retirement savings in cash, 10% in a basic fixed-index annuity, 10% in a fixed-index annuity, tied to stock and bond performance, 25% in a guaranteed lifetime withdrawal benefit (GLWB) product[13], 20% in bonds and 30% in the global stock market. What is this investor's risk level?

Assuming bonds are flat, meaning they don't lose value when the stock

---

13   According to Investopedia, A rider on a variable annuity that allows minimum withdrawals from the invested amount without having to annuitize the investment. The amount that can be withdrawn is based on a percentage of the total amount invested in the annuity. The GLWB will be discussed in more depth on page 81.

markets are down, this becomes a simple numbers problem to solve. Let's say the stock market crashed 30% in a given year! How much would this portfolio lose?

We learned earlier that fixed-index annuities and GLWBs can't lose value; cash can't lose. When stocks are down, bonds are likely to gain, but we are assuming no change. This leaves the 25% in the stock market investment as the only asset that decreases in value. If this portion lost 30%, your loss would be 7.5% of your overall portfolio.

If this is too high, given a market crash, perhaps your investment strategy is too risky. If 7.5% is no big deal, perhaps you need to take on higher risk for the potential of higher return.

The point here is that it is possible to quantify the amount of risk you are taking given a market correction. Equally important is to determine the percentage increase of your portfolio given a market increase.

Let's say the market increased 30% in a given year. Would you be okay with a 15% return knowing you were also protected against a devastating market drop? These are the critical questions when analyzing your personal risk tolerance. Also know that spouses rarely share the same tolerance for risk, and that needs to be taken into account.

It's times like these that I'm happy I have a great big math trophy.

PART TWO: LIVE BETTER

The Estate Planning and Tax Efficiency Process begins with a well thought out and constructed financial plan. The plan will integrate these two areas while also accounting for your pre- and post-retirement needs. By the nature of such a plan, there is a lot of crossover into the various sections of the plan. It is important to have well-qualified professionals working together to maximize your benefits.

Often, it is the financial advisor/RIA that coordinates both the CPA and EPA (Estate Planning Attorney) and provides the "home base" for making sure that everything works together for your good. A good RIA will keep the plan moving forward and will be the glue that makes the plan stick to your needs and goals.

Ultimately, when the plan is completed and underway you have a dynamic document that not only accounts for your wishes but will be monitored throughout your life, and your spouse's, if you are married. The plan provides clarity, confidence, and continuity about your finances and estate, leaving you free to focus on living.

> *Dale: My dad was a very pragmatic person and he would remind me often, "Son you make a living the best way you know how and pay others to do the same. This advice will save you a lot of time and money through the years."*

HOW TO FIND THE RIGHT PLANNING PROFESSIONALS

When it comes to retirement, estate, and tax planning, Dale's father's advice could not be more true. Hire professionals through reputable sources to manage these areas of your finances. They are typically well-read on the latest in their respective industry, well-educated in their field, and finally, well-suited to provide you with the products and services necessary for your personal financial success.

Avoid on-line reviews offered through referral sources. These reviews are often paid for or sponsored ads. If you have not been referred through someone that you currently know, I would avoid employing that reference.

Other on-line resources to avoid are do-it-yourself legal documents.

They can leave you woefully short in the areas that you are deploying these of the documents. We have found that there are also additional documents required to fully facilitate the protection you desire. For example, Living Trusts require the funding of the trust and this requires that additional paperwork be completed and filed.

TAXES

Taxes are one of the single largest expenses we have, yet we spend so little time considering ways we can keep Uncle Sam out of our wallets.

Every financial move you make has tax implications. When you have a professional team of seasoned experts monitoring those tax consequences and offering strategic advice in concert with your investment management, retirement and estate planning, your savings could be staggering.

TRUSTS

In this chapter, and in other chapters in this book, we will discuss trusts. But what is a trust, and what is its purpose?

The most basic reason to establish a trust is to help someone carry out their wishes even after they are unable to do so, or after they have passed away. Trusts can be set up to do lots of things:

- Protect assets from tax
- Assist spouses and children by providing qualified decision makers
- Provide for disabled children in case you can no longer be there to care for them, or
- Help ensure children or charities of your choice receive your assets upon your passing

Tax Tail Wagging the Dog

When I say the tax tail wags the dog, I'm referring to making decisions solely based on tax implications even when the decision flies in the face of good overall sense.

I have been asked many times to give my opinion on the decision of whether it makes sense to pay off the primary residential mortgage early. These situations occur when the homeowner expects to live in the house for an extended period of time, has a high equity percentage, and has ample funds to pay it off. Most of the time, the client asking me this question doesn't think they should pay it off. They think they "need" the tax write-off.

One day a client presented me with a situation just like that. After doing an inventory of all their assets and liabilities, they wanted my advice on how to invest their money. They had $150,000 in cash but their caveat was that they did not want to lose any of the principal of this investment. They didn't plan on needing these funds for many years to come. With CD rates hovering under 1% at the time, they didn't think they had any real options.

I asked them if they would like a 5% guaranteed rate of return with no risk of loss. They laughed and said, "sure, we would do that in a heart-beat." I said, "You have a $130,000 mortgage at 5%. By using your cash money to pay off the mortgage, you could guarantee saving 5% on it, and saving money is really the same as making money."

They said that wouldn't make sense because they would be losing all their write-offs. I explained that at 5%, they are paying about $6,500 per year in mortgage payments. Those mortgage interest payments, along with their other itemized deductions were barely above the Standard Deduction they can claim on their tax return. In this case, the loss of the mortgage write-off really only amounted to a couple hundred dollars. After comparing a few hundred dollars to the 5% "guaranteed" return, along with the piece-of-mind of having their residence paid off, they immediately brightened up at the prospect.

An interesting side note. They then said, "We came in asking you to invest our money, yet you told us to pay off our mortgage. How do you get paid on that advice?"

I replied, "I don't get paid on it, but I'm a fiduciary and all I have to do is give the best answers I can to each situation."

"That's awesome", is all they had to say to that.

Proceeds and Cash Flow and Gains, Oh My!

Congratulations! You just sold your rental home and you're ready to move on to the next chapter. You found the perfect beach view condo in Maui for $350,000 that you should just be able to afford with the cash from your house

Hopefully.

Do you know what you'll have in your pocket when the deal is done? "Of course," you say, "I just take the selling price and deduct my mortgage payoff, right?"

Your house is worth $750,000 and you owe less than $400,000. This seems simple enough.

Well, it's not so simple. There are different taxation rules for primary residences, second residences, and rentals. In addition to income tax consequences, you need to factor in closing costs and the confusing concept called "basis."

Rather than writing a War and Peace-length chapter explaining all these nuances, I'd like to offer one example of selling a rental house to try to shed some light on these. Ideally, you'll speak to a good CPA before making large transactions.

Often when people are selling rental property they don't fully understand the terms cash flow, proceeds, and taxable gains and how these relate to their bottom line.

Cash flow is the money in your pocket once the deal is done.

Gross proceeds is the full amount the buyer is willing to pay. Many people forget to subtract closing costs from this number to arrive at their net proceeds from the sale.

In addition, you must pay income tax based on your taxable gain when selling rental property, which may not be the case in a primary residence, and this tax must also be subtracted from your net proceeds before you can finally arrive at the actual amount of money in your pocket (net cash).

Basis can be a confusing concept, but is important for determining what you will be taxed on. If you purchased the property for $400,000, this is your initial basis. If you put an addition on that costs $100,000, your basis is now $500,000. Since it was a rental property, you took a depreciation deduction each year which incrementally reduced your basis figure over time.

It's now 10 years later and you're ready to sell. Let's assume you took out an equity loan some years back and your remaining mortgage balance is $397,045 and the sales price is $750,000. Your taxable gain is calculated as follows:

Basis before adjustments	$ 500,000
Less accumulated depreciation	(181,818)
Plus closing costs @ 8%	60,000
Adjusted basis	$ 378,182
Gross proceeds	$ 750,000
Less adjusted basis	(378,182)
Taxable Gain	$ 371,818

However this is not the net cash that you will walk away with. Paying off a mortgage when a property is sold does not reduce your taxable gain—but it does reduce the net cash you have in your pocket. Your net cash will be:

Gross Proceeds	$ 750,000
Less remaining mortgage	(397,045)
Less closing costs	(60,000)
Less tax on gain*	(92,955)
Net proceeds (cash in pocket)	$ 200,000

Now you know if you can be on the beach in Maui or if you should start looking in Arizona instead.

* The gain may be excludable if the home was your primary residence for 2 of the last 5 years before it was sold. For this example we used an arbitrary 25% effective tax rate.

I WANT IT NOW!

In the movie *Willy Wonka and the Chocolate Factory,* one of the Golden Ticket winners touring the Chocolate Factory was Veruca Salt, heiress to the Salt nut fortune and a real brat. When Veruca doesn't get what she wants immediately, she acts out until she finally wears down all opposition to her selfish demands.

In a key scene, Veruca sings a song with the constant refrain, "Give it to me now!"

"Give it to me now" doesn't work in the real world, especially with the IRS. During your working life, you will probably have money withheld by your employer from your paycheck and remitted to the IRS on your behalf. This is likely to be enough to cover your income taxes for that year, maybe with a little refund (woo-hoo). The IRS gets the funds throughout the year as you get paid.

They get it now!

So what happens if you don't get a paycheck? What if you're self-employed? What if you're retired? You can just pay your taxes in April when you file your return, right? WRONG!

They want it now!

When you don't have an employer remitting to the IRS on your behalf every pay period, the IRS requires you to make quarterly estimated tax payments throughout the year due April 15, June 15, September 15 and January 15 to avoid penalties and interest.[14] This is also true for retired persons. No withholding from your retirement and investment income? Better think about quarterly payments in your retirement planning.

They want it now!

For instance, I get a call from a retired client who needs $50,000 for a new car and they request $50,000 from their IRA. I then remind them of their 25% marginal tax bracket and that they need to take out $67,000 in order to cover the taxes now. That car just got a whole lot more expensive.

---

14   There are also "safe harbor" amounts that are based on the prior year tax that can help you avoid quarterly recalculations of your income – but you still need to make the payments quarterly!

A common mistake in estimating income tax for self-employed individuals is not realizing that, as far as the IRS is concerned, you are the employer *and* the employee for payroll taxes. You need to pay both portions of the Medicare and Social Security taxes, over 15% of your business profits.

Let's assume you started a successful new business that nets $100,000 per year. You didn't make tax estimates the first year. Let's also assume your average income tax on these earnings is 20%. In April of the next year, your CPA informs you that you now owe $35,000 in combined income and self employment tax *and* you need to make another $35,000 for current year estimated taxes. This adds up to more than what you expect in profit for the entire rest of the year!

They want it now!

The other pitfall for making timely payments is in regards to tax return extensions. Filing an extension can often be necessary to gather the information needed to complete your return. But that's all it is! An extension does not extend your time to pay your taxes. The extension only extends your time to file. You still must pay all taxes you expect to owe by April 15th to avoid penalties and interest.

They want it now!

FOUR FLAVORS OF TAX

As if Basis Tax Law weren't confusing enough, now I'm talking tax flavors?

This chapter may seem basic, but many people still struggle with understanding the basic definitions of tax ramifications.

The four flavors of tax:

1. A tax deduction is not a tax credit. This is the most common misconception I hear. For instance, how many times have we heard someone dismiss how much something costs by claiming, "it doesn't matter, it's deductible." Well, it does matter. A deduction can only offset a portion of the cost equal to your marginal tax bracket. So if your marginal rate is 25%, every $100 you spend in deductible items can only get you $25 back at the most. So you are still out the $75.

    Marginal tax rates are only the rate of tax we will pay on any additional dollars earned. Let's say you make $100,000 in a year and your marginal tax rate is 28%. Many people assume they are paying $28,000 in income tax. The reality is that some of you are taxed at lower rates, thanks to exemptions and itemized or standard deductions. Many taxpayers pay an average rate of 12% to 15% on their total income.

2. A tax credit, as opposed to a tax deduction, is a dollar-for-dollar benefit. Here, a $100 credit really is worth $100, as opposed to the $25 in the previous example for a deduction. Are all tax deductible items going to get you a tax refund at your marginal rate? The answer is "no." Many so-called tax deductible items like tax preparation fees or medical costs have significant restrictions on their ability to offer you any true tax relief. Other deductions like passive losses or larger charitable donations may only be deductible in a future year through the use of carry forwards of these amounts.

3. Tax-deferred earnings will some day require the tax to be paid. For instance, earnings in your 401(k) plan are tax

deferred.

4. <u>Tax free is something completely different.</u> If you sell your residence at a gain of say $100,000, this gain may be tax free, meaning nobody will ever pay tax on it.

The Shawshank Redemption, Clarified

This is one of my all-time favorite movies. You may remember the scene when the inmates were on the roof and the evil guard was bemoaning an inheritance because the taxes would just take it all away. Then Andy Dufresne asked him if he trusted his wife. That question almost cost Andy his life until Andy went on to explain how a one-time gift to his spouse could help the guard avoid the tax.

Actually, there is no Federal Inheritance Tax.

When someone dies, all of the asset values are computed. If the assets are very high (in 2015 it is above $5.25 million), there is a Federal Estate Tax. Assuming in this example, there is a taxable estate, the tax would be paid out of the estate assets prior to the distribution of these assets by the executor.

With the exception of possible income taxes due from inherited retirement accounts and annuities, the inheritor does not owe any inheritance tax. Any estate tax owed should be paid out of the estate, and the inheritance is out of the net after-tax assets.

In addition, refer to the chapter titled "Step On Up" and you may not even owe income tax when you sell appreciated property. To be perfectly honest, dying is one of the most effective tax planning strategies, but still, I highly advise against it!

I am glad Andy Dufresne didn't tell the guard about the inheritance tax rules. The movie would never have turned out so interesting without this critical scene!

PART THREE: RETIRE BETTER

Today, you face new challenges that no other generation has faced before when retiring. With everything that has happened on Wall Street since the turn of the century, many people and their portfolios have been left vulnerable in this fast-paced financial environment.

Navigating this on your own can be confusing. Pension plans have gone by the wayside and retirees are faced with the challenge of creating their own "paycheck" from their savings for upwards of 30 years of life expectancy.

Working with your team of CPA, RIA and EPA, develop a plan that will:

- Make sure you will get the most out of Social Security
- Preserve your wealth by reducing exposure to future market downturns
- Create a reliable income stream that will last through retirement

These questions from our proprietary (but free-for-the-asking) *The Madrona Life and Legacy Planner* will help you get started with your planning team.

GENERAL PLANNING

	Y	N
Do you have a Will?	☐	☐
When was it last updated? _____/_____/_____		
Do you have a Living Trust?	☐	☐
When was it last updated? _____/_____/_____		
Have you designated the distribution of personal property to heirs?	Y	N
Do you receive any trust income?	Y	N
Do you expect to be named beneficiary of a trust or will (inheritance)?	Y	N
Does your family know the location of your Will?	Y	N
Does your family know the location of your Living Trust?	Y	N
Are you worried that there may be disagreements between family members after your passing when it comes to dealing with your estate?	Y	N

GENERAL PLANNING

| Do you have a financial guardian appointed for your children (if applicable)? | Y ☐ | N ☐ |
| Have you determined who will care for your children if something happens to you? | Y ☐ | N ☐ |

If so, who? _____

Do you have an up-to-date comprehensive inventory of your household, furnishings or possesions?	Y ☐	N ☐
Do you periodically prepare a personal balance sheet (i.e. assets and liabilities)?	Y ☐	N ☐
Do you periodically prepare a budget that lists income and expenses?	Y ☐	N ☐
What amount of emergency cash reserves do you prefer to have set aside?	$ _____	
Do you expect your spouse to continue working?	Y ☐	N ☐
Do you plan on making any significant contributions to charity at any point?	Y ☐	N ☐

FAMILY ADVISORS

Title	Name	Phone	Email
CPA - Accountant			
Attorney			
Banker			
Insurance Agent			
Financial Advisor			
Stockbroker			
Trust Officer			

MUSIC LESSONS

We are both music lovers. We love all genres. One of the popular songs we listened to while growing up was by the group Supertramp called, "Take the Long Way Home."

The song is somewhat dark and depressing but the title itself speaks of a journey, one that suggests that we not rush to get to where we are going.

Retirement is better when you have the means to live well throughout your sojourning until that day you make it home to your final place of rest. None of us knows when that time will come but given good health, most will agree that the longer we have to spend with loved ones, the better.

Taking the long way home then, for each of us, becomes a costly proposition as we will spend a lot of money, more than most of us will plan for in our pre-retirement years. If we are to travel the long road of retirement home—and in fact plan to retire better—it is necessary to set a realistic budget for our retirement expenses so that our finances will last as long as we do.

What we have learned in working with clients is that when it comes to their retirement, the quality of their retirement years is most often determined by how much of the could-haves (defined below) they get to enjoy, and not their household and transportation items. When faced with decisions such as whether to enjoy all of their elective items or their household, they will cut the household somehow, somewhere, nearly every time.

The decisions look like, "We can sell the house and move to a condo so that we can help fund our yearly travel," or, "Let's sell the 6,000 square-foot house since our children are grown up and have moved out, and downsize—this way we can help the grandchildren out with college expenses."

Effective retirement budgets are broken into three groups: Must-haves, Should-haves, and Could-haves.

Must-have items in your budget are those that you determine are necessary for your retirement enjoyment—these are qualitative decisions.

One retiree may need to have a house to live in while another is comfortable with a small condominium. Still another may need to domicile in Hawaii while someone else chooses Kansas.

One of my clients never made more than $50,000/year, retired a millionaire and is able to live on $45,000/year, while another multi-millionaire chooses to live on three times that amount. There is no wrong choice except for the one that you cannot afford. Qualify your must-haves and then select the should-haves of your retirement.

MUST-HAVE (NECESSARY)

Living/Household Expenses
Transportation
Taxes

Should-have items in your budget convey prudence in your planning and are illustrated best by considering insurances. Not all insurance is necessary—some kinds are more necessary than others—and there are varying coverage amounts for your final consideration.

These are often quantitative decisions—you are choosing to be prudent and therefore deciding on how much coverage and the size of deductibles to get, not whether you should remain exposed for liability. Your should-haves flow from your must-haves in the retirement planning process, and should be quantified prior to your could-have decisions.

SHOULD-HAVE (PRUDENT)

Long-Term Care Insurance
Medicare Supplemental Insurance
Appropriate Amount of Life Insurance

Could-have items are elective in nature and accordingly, can be either qualitative or quantitative. You can want more or better or both. You may choose to live in a house and have it on the beach in Hawaii.

If you "could have" your preferences what would they be? This is truly the fun area of the retirement planning process because it forces all of us to begin with the end in mind.

When you have arrived home, what will you have wanted your journey to include? Once you can fully answer this question it's time to evaluate the efficacy of your plan by reviewing the total arrangement working backwards.

COULD-HAVE (ELECTIVE)

Grandchild's Education Expense
Gifts
Charitable Giving
(Possibly be Must-have or Should-have depending on beliefs)
Vacation
Plastic Surgery
Country Club Membership
Entertainment

Take a look at the could-haves first. Is the list comprehensive and does it contain all of the items that you would like to include in your retirement?

Once the list is complete, move on to your should-haves and review this list in a similar fashion. Is everything that you find prudent for your retirement listed? If not, complete the list and move on to the must-haves and finish your overall evaluation.

Once you have the finished plan, it's time to assess it for feasibility.

Your plan is both feasible and practical if you can pay for the plan starting with the elective items first, then the prudent, and finally, the necessary.

Why do we plan this way? Because we know that in order to take the enjoyable and long way home through retirement, you must be able to possess the could-haves along the way (or you will feel like you are just existing and not living).

So we have you start there, at the most enjoyable part of your retirement preparation. Do you have enough money to acquire your could-haves independent of the should-haves and must-haves? If so, great, move on to the should-haves and finally the must-haves doing a similar assessment at each point.

The idea here is to obviously have enough money in retirement to cover all of these expenses throughout your retirement beginning with your could-haves.

If you find that at some point in your analysis you are short of funds, it is time to reevaluate the must-haves.

Most people who do retirement planning allocate money first for their necessary expenses, then the prudent, and if any money is left over, they fund a portion of their elective choices with the remaining finances. They may be able to play bridge weekly and enjoy lunch out with their friends but they are not able to travel as frequently as they prefer.

Starting with your electives and finishing the retirement planning process by evaluating what you thought was necessary brings your retirement into focus and provides for what is hopefully, a long journey home.

CHRISTMAS MORNING OR CHRISTMAS EVE?

Growing up, I couldn't wait for Christmas morning. The anticipation of seeing what was under the tree for me was almost more than I could take.

I was jealous of my friends who were allowed to open their presents on Christmas Eve. You understand what I mean, right?

Do you open your Christmas presents on Christmas Eve or Christmas morning? There is no right or wrong answer to this question but I bet that your answer has something to do with your family traditions.

The truth is, it doesn't matter what day you open the presents—what is yours under the tree will be yours when you get around to opening them. The same is not necessarily true regarding your retirement savings—you may lose some to Uncle Sam depending on how you choose to take withdrawals from the accounts.

Assuming you have both tax-qualified savings accounts (IRA, 403(b), etc.) and non-qualified accounts, the manner in which you choose to liquidate your holdings in retirement may have a significant impact on your net withdrawals (after taxes).

The goal of course, is to maximize the amount of money you retain versus how much is paid to Uncle Sam. Unlike when you open Christmas presents, there is a preferred solution that works for most people in the majority of cases.

To optimize your "take home" (after taxes) amount in retirement start by deciding when you will begin to receive your Social Security (SS) benefits and make your withdrawals from your retirement accounts. The longer you can wait on receiving your SS benefit, the greater your potential gain. Following the schedule below will help you net the most after-tax benefit:[15]

- Delay claiming your SS benefits until age 70
- Delaying SS until age 70 yields a guaranteed 8% per year

---

15   Seek advice from a CPA about your specific situation

in delayed credits

- Withdraw from your tax-qualified accounts first
- Couple your SS benefits and withdrawals from your non-qualified investments at age 70

DOES CONGRESS HATE OLD PEOPLE?

The topic is called Required Minimum Distributions. The concept is fairly simple, but the ramifications and execution are not.

When funds are left in retirement plans, the IRS can't collect taxes. Laws were passed requiring older people to take money out of their plans annually so income taxes could be collected. Simple enough, right?

The law was passed requiring amounts to be withdrawn based on an actuarial table, rather than set percentages. Then, the start date was determined to be the year in which we turn 70½ or the year following the year we turn 70½.

My nine-year-old son could have come up with something more logical than this, but it's the next part that really gripes me.

Let's say Aunt Gladys has a Required Minimum Distribution (RMD) of $80,000. Aunt Gladys has been having problems with early dementia and she forgets to withdraw the money from her retirement plans in time, so she took her withdrawal a month late. Congress is very good at one thing—figuring out penalties. In the case of RMDs, they actually made it rather simple. Instead of owing interest, Aunt Gladys has a simple 50% penalty to pay. So by being a month late to move her own money from one account to another, she owes a $40,000 penalty! This is one of the heaviest penalties imposed by congressional rule.

My editorial comment is that this rule is absurd and is aimed at citizens in their weakest state. This is a penalty that should be struck from the tax code. Here's something practical you can do for Aunt Gladys: work with her CPA to be sure she gets a reminder 45 days ahead of her birthday. Most importantly, this is another reason why all three advisors (CPA, RIA, and EPA) should be working together.

CHRISTIANS, MECHANICS, AND YOUR 401(K)

Look, just because someone may go to church on occasion, this fact alone does not make them a Christian. Similarly, I own a garage and many tools, but I can assure you that I will never be mistaken for a mechanic. Yet all of us who participate in 401(k) plans are required to self-direct our investments and essentially be "asset allocation" experts when it comes to our primary retirement fund.

Does this make any sense?

Clients of mine are often embarrassed that they don't understand the markets or the tax code. They see commercials of babies easily maneuvering their stock portfolios or commercials saying the computer can easily solve all your tax preparation questions. Neither of these assertions is remotely true. I have spent 30 years learning my trade. Why expect yourself to easily pick up this kind of experience?

It used to be that many workers would stay at a job their whole career and then upon retirement, would receive a defined benefit pension paying them for the rest of their lives. With the advent of 401(k)s, the burden of investing has been transferred to us as employees, yet most workers have very little experience building proper risk-adjusted asset allocation models. Even fewer of us know what an asset allocation model even is. In addition, most plans have high fees and/ or very limited investment choices.

Besides getting help from an experi-

UNDERSTANDING YOUR 401(K) OPTIONS AT 59 ½

Consider In-Service, Non-Hardship Withdrawals for:

1. Creating Better Income Solutions
2. Providing Investment Options
3. Plan Consolidations
4. Offering More Beneficiary Options
5. Stretching IRA
6. Protecting Principal

Be sure to get professional help

enced financial planner, what can someone do about this? If you are 59 ½ your plan may allow for something called "non-hardship, in-service distributions." This is where you set up your own IRA, and roll some or all of your current balance into it. This is a tax-free transfer.

Then, instead of only having 10-30 choices for your investments, you now have thousands. In addition, you can now take advantage of some of the lower-risk insurance company investment options.

Finally, you can still continue to contribute to your existing 401(k) plan, and receive any employer match.

This is a complex area of the tax code and there are some potential advantages to leaving funds in a plan after 59 ½, but often the disadvantages can outweigh this.

MAKING LIFE INSURANCE LESS CONFUSING

Life insurance is a confusing concept for many of our clients. The confusion starts with the name "life" insurance because these policies don't pay out their benefit until someone is dead. The marketing and advertising people probably got it right though, because "death insurance" isn't a very marketable term!

In our experience, we have found that life insurance isn't something every person needs. It is generally a good idea to insure your life when you have dependents, or when the loss of your income may be financially devastating to someone else.

For someone without heirs, an older and financially-secure couple, or for a college student, it is seldom necessary. There are those who would argue that getting a very small term policy on a dependent child makes sense, if for no better reason that to preserve insurability for when they do take on responsibilities. In these cases, we recommend no more than is required to cover the insured child's burial expenses.

TERM INSURANCE

Basic life insurance is called "term insurance." This is by far the cheapest of all policies because it just pays a death benefit and rarely has any other features.

A potential problem with term insurance is that you typically can purchase it only for a set term of years. Let's say you are 30 years old, and you have young children. You may purchase an inexpensive term policy for a term of 30 years to help in the case of your early passing, before your family can support itself.

In our experience, life insurance makes sense for folks who have dependents who cannot support themselves. Young families come to mind as well as families with one breadwinner and insufficient savings and investments to support the family in the event the breadwinner dies prematurely. Buying a 30-year term policy at age 30 will get most families through the time when they are at greatest risk of premature death. Once the policy expires, you might be able to qualify for another term policy, but the cost of a policy for a 60-year-old will be substantial.

With each passing year, the cost of insurance increases, so we recommend getting a policy with a fixed premium for the term of the policy, which can be as few as five years and greater than 30 years, as in the example above. Some policies come with provisions to renew the term policy at pre-determined rates, and these policies will cost more than those without such guarantees.

PERMANENT INSURANCE

It's easy to think of life insurance products as being either term or permanent. There are lots of products called lots of different names that are permanent life insurance. If you encounter policies with names like whole life, universal life, variable life, indexed universal life, etc., these policies can be many times the cost of a term insurance policy. When you break them down, they will resemble the combination of a lifetime term policy along with an investment component.

The investment component depends on the policy type.

- A whole life policy is analogous to term insurance plus a fixed annuity
- A variable life policy is analogous to term insurance plus a variable annuity
- Indexed universal life is somewhat like term insurance plus an indexed annuity

As you age, the cost of insurance in your policy can increase dramatically, as we said earlier. If you are paying a fixed premium on a form of permanent insurance, and the death benefit does not change, then over time you are decreasing your investment value in the policy.

Before you buy permanent insurance, make sure to understand your reasons for doing so. Insurance can be an important estate planning tool, but if you are really only looking for good investments as well as life insurance for a certain period of time, then you may want to consider a term policy while investing outside of permanent insurance.

Beware the zealous sales person. Most insurance agents want you to buy permanent insurance, not term. Why is this? Follow the money: commissions on term policies are lower than those on permanent policies. If you decide to go with a policy that combines a death benefit with insurance features, know why you are combining the two. It doesn't always make sense to do so.

FIXED-INDEX ANNUITIES

Where does someone go to earn reasonable returns without taking on excessive risk? One answer lies outside of Wall Street, but instead with an insurance company product.

Here is an example of someone who went in that direction. Betty was traumatized by the market crash in the early 2000s and wanted some real protection of her principal. She purchased a fixed-index annuity and opted for the crediting method called the "annual point-to-point tied to the S&P 500 Index" on July 1, 2008 for $100,000. Note that date.

This product measures the change in the S&P 500 from the date of purchase until one year later and she receives that percentage change, but with two exceptions. First, she has a floor of 0% and a ceiling of 6% in this example.

The market crashed three months after she bought the policy. So the first year, the market decline means the value of her account stayed at $100,000. In the years following, if the S&P gained 4%, she would get the 4%. If it gained 14% she is capped at 6%, and receives that. This particular example assumes she doesn't cash this investment out in the first seven years. Otherwise a surrender penalty would apply.

So Betty gets to receive some market returns, will never lose value and brags to her friends that she did just fine in the crash of 2008!

This type of investment is becoming very popular due to low CD and money market returns currently. It is also quite popular for a percentage of retirees' portfolios since the product cannot lose value in a particular year.

Fixed index annuities, like all insurance company products, carry some degree of risk, but less risk than the products of most other financial institutions. The odds of insurer insolvency occurring is historically very slim. Additionally, the chances of a policyholder "losing it all" in such a scenario even slimmer, given the numerous and robust regulatory backstops to insurer insolvency.

"It's very, very rare for a life insurer to become insolvent," says Michael Barry, spokesman for the Insurance Information Institute, an industry trade group. "Life insurers are among the best capitalized insurance companies out there."[16]

Indeed, just 80 multi-state life and health insurers and 326 single-state or regional insurers have failed over the past four decades. Life insurers performed particularly well during the recent recession, with just eight insolvencies between 2008 and 2012. Not only did those companies' combined liability of $900 million pale in comparison to the $639 billion Lehman Brothers bankruptcy, most policyholders recovered all or nearly all benefits under contract.

If the insurance company issuing the policy fails, the policy holder must rely on external guarantees. Most states have an insurance guarantee fund for payouts in the case of an insurance company policy. They differ from state to state. The policy will only mitigate your loss, not make you whole. In California, for example, an insurance policy or annuity owner will receive 80% of any one policy up to $250,000. Therefore, on a $400,000 policy the most you would get is 80%, with a per person maximum of $300,000.

One of these guarantees exists in my home state of Washington. Generally, policies are insured by the Tate Guarantee Fund for up to $500,000 per company. In any case, make sure you are invested with a highly rated insurance carrier. We recommend following the ratings of A.M. Best and not purchasing a policy rated below B+.

---

16   "Help! My life insurance company went broke," BankRate.com, last accessed January 12, 2015. http://www.bankrate.com/finance/insurance/life-insurance-company-went-broke.aspx

More? Better!

Chances are that if you have worked most of your life and paid into the Social Security system, you are looking forward to receiving a monthly check sooner or later. Hypothetically speaking, if you were expecting a check for $2,100 per month but instead, could realize monthly payments of $2,300-$2,400, you would choose the greater. Why? Simple! More is better!

But as AARP reports[17], there will be 8,000 people turning 65 every day for the next 18 years in the United State. Many are retiring and leaving tens of thousands of dollars in lifetime benefits on the table.

By employing legal and often obscure or misunderstood strategies, retirees can maximize their monthly and ultimately, lifetime benefits—a difference that can add up to over $100,000 for a couple.

While we could write an entire book on Social Security, we simply want people to recognize that it is one of their greatest investments and that there is much at stake relative to how and when they elect to receive it. We strongly advise that you consult with a professional advi-

Here's a quick selection of terms you will encounter when researching and dealing with Social Security:

The Old-Age, Survivors, and Disability Insurance (OASDI) Program, which for most of us means "Social Security," is intended to provide monthly benefits to partially replace lost income due to retirement, death, or disability.

Full Retirement Age (FRA), when a worker can receive an unreduced benefit, varies according to date of birth and generally ranges from age 65-67.

The Primary Insurance Amount (PIA), or monthly benefit, is tied solely to a person's work record—the 35 highest earnings years are used to calculate benefits.

The Windfall Elimination Provision (WEP) and the Government Pension Offset (GPO) pertain to persons receiving non-covered (employed by employers who did not withhold Social Security taxes such as government agencies, state colleges, etc.) pensions. Those receiving this type of pension may (most likely will) have their PIA reduced. In the case of the GPO, spousal and survivor benefits will be reduced by ⅔ of the non-covered pension. In both cases of non-covered pensions, Social Security may adjust benefits for those entitled to them.

---

17   "Baby Boomers Turning 65," AARP, last accessed January 12, 2015. http://www.aarp.org/personal-growth/transitions/boomers_65/

sor concerning this topic.

The choice of "how" to receive benefits is equally important as to "when" retirees are going to elect their Social Security benefits. There are multiple choices available to individuals, and hundreds to choose from for married couples and qualified domestic partners (see your state law).

The problem for many, though, is how to determine what strategy will yield them and their household the most money. What is best for one couple may not be right for another. Making your best choice starts with knowing what you don't know.

There are many factors to consider when deciding what the most appropriate time and method is for claiming OASDI benefits. Some of the issues are easily considered such as: retirement goals, current health, family health history, retirement assets, needs and budget, and other factors affecting longevity.

Most important in assessing your decision to collect Social Security, is understanding at what point you can no longer live comfortably due to retirement, disability, or the death of a spouse.

Maximizing your lifetime benefits from Social Security provides the maximum payment for the length of time that you and your household need it.

You may want to consult with a financial advisor to request your personalized "Social Security Maximization Report" for your unique situation. This report incorporates your and your spouse's (if applicable) earnings histories as reported on your Social Security Statement and is available at www.socialsecurity.gov/myaccount.

I'm Older, Can I Afford to See the Doctor?

Unless you are like Brian's dad, who won't go to a doctor unless he can see the broken bone as it pokes through his skin, most of us visit the doctor more often as we age. So the question I'm often asked is whether health care costs will send a retiree to the proverbial poor house.

Prior to the age of 65, it's important to have adequate health insurance, preferably through your employer. Medicare is available to you at age 65 regardless of your health. The cost is predetermined and may be adjusted based on your income. Medicare only covers certain health care costs as it is somewhat limited in coverage.

To fill this coverage gap, you need to purchase a Medicare supplement plan (or Medi-Gap policy). The website Medicare.gov offers easy-to-understand explanations and we can do no better than to refer you there to understand your options.[18]

Why do we recommend both Medicare Supplement? The plans are standardized, so really, you only have to pick the plan that suits your situation. The more the policy covers, the more it costs. However the cost of these policies is really quite reasonable.

Chart One (see next page) is the supplemental policy chart. As you can see, Plan F carries the most coverage.

---

18   "What's Medicare Supplement Insurance (Medigap)?" Medicare.gov, last accessed January 12, 2015.

Benefits	Medicare Supplement Insurance Plans (Medigap)									
	A	B	C	D	F*	G	K	L	M	N
Medicare Part A Coinsurance and Hospital Costs (up to an additional 365 days after Medicare benefits are used)	√	√	√	√	√	√	√	√	√	√
Medicare Part B Coinsurance or Copayment	√	√	√	√	√	√	50%	75%	√	√**
Blood (first 3 pints)	√	√	√	√	√	√	50%	75%	√	√
Part A Hospice Care Coinsurance or Copayment	√	√	√	√	√	√	50%	75%	√	√
Skilled Nursing Facility Care Coinsurance			√	√	√	√	50%	75%	√	√
Medicare Part A Deductible		√	√	√	√	√	50%	75%	50%	√
Medicare Part B Deductible			√		√					
Medicare Part B Excess Charges					√	√				
Foreign Travel Emergency (up to plan limits)			√	√	√	√			√	√
Out-of-Pocket Limit							$4,640	$2,320		

The second option is to purchase a Medicate Advantage policy. The Medicate Advantage combines all coverage into one comprehensive plan. Medi-gap policies work much like an HMO. However, these plans may limit your choice of doctors

Insurance Meets Wall Street

We covered some annuity questions earlier, but we didn't fully address another type of annuity called the "variable annuity." More people buy this than any other kind of annuity. Some items sell well because they are the best. Others sell well because a great deal of effort is put into the sale. This is a case of the latter.

The concept of the variable annuity is to invest money in the stock market, long term, without the risk of losing money. So let's say you invests $100,000 in a variable annuity and holds it for 15 years. During that time, you would select various investments with the insurance company. These investments would return to you your $100,000, no matter what happens in the market.

Sounds pretty good, but what is the catch?

The main catch is the fees that impose a significant drag on your investment account. Often these fees exceed 3% per year. Therefore, over the course of 15 years, the compound effect of fees at 3% could decrease your account value by 50% or more.

If that weren't tough enough to stomach, you have to become your own investment advisor by selecting your own investments from the menu of products offered. You are also responsible for monitoring your choices.

So why are variable annuities the best-selling annuity on the market? Maybe just "follow the money." You see, variable annuities offer some of the highest commissions in the financial services industry.

Sometimes these products are a perfect fit, but you must examine the motives and alternatives behind the sales process of this product. We believe these are among the most oversold financial products on the market today. We also know that there are other ways to reduce risk and put together an investment plan that works as well or better than this one.

YOU CAN'T SPEND DIRT

As I mentioned previously, cash flow is of paramount importance in retirement. Eventually, real estate or partnerships must be turned into something more liquid to live on. But here is another potential problem in retirement most people haven't considered: what if you live too long and are too healthy?

No, that was not a typo. Living too long can mean outliving your money especially given the effects of inflation. If you retire at 62 years old and live to be 97, do you really have enough assets saved to live on for 35 years?

And what about being too healthy and active? Most people dramatically slow down their spending as they age due to normal health issues and a decrease in overall activity. But some people remain quite vibrant into their 80's or 90's, continue to travel, maintain their house and remain very active, experiencing no significant slowdown in their lifestyle or spending habits.

Maybe you have Social Security along with a lifetime pension from work. Fewer and fewer people have pensions, but instead have 401(k) accounts. Did you know it's possible to essentially "buy a pension" with 401(k) assets, IRAs or non-retirement assets?

The insurance industry calls this a guaranteed lifetime withdrawal benefit, which can have even better attributes than a standard pension. The "guaranteed lifetime withdrawal benefit" is a rider to a fixed-index annuity, which we discussed in Part One: Invest Better.

For example, Bill and his wife Betty do not have a pension, but both have longevity in their families and want to not only reduce market risk (the risk of loss in the stock market), but also longevity risk (the risk of outliving your money).

Bill decides at age 60 to invest retirement money into a fixed-index annuity. The product allows their investment to grow with the stock and bond market returns in years where the markets increase. When the markets go down, their investment account does not.

Years after the investment, Bill decides to turn on the lifetime cash flow payments. Once started, these payments continue as long as either

Bill or Betty are alive, no matter how long that is. In some cases, these payments increase over the years. Finally, if both Bill and Betty die prematurely, the remaining balance in their underlying investment account can go to their heirs.

Using a "guaranteed lifetime withdrawal benefit" can be an important part of a retirement plan since it can provide growth, cash flow, inflation solutions, and protection.

Dale: Reflections on the Death of my Uninsured Father

Life changed for my entire family on March 8, 1991.

Although I lived in California, I was traveling in Washington state when I got word that my dad had collapsed on the treadmill while undergoing a stress test. Fortunately, I was with my wife's sister and her husband Brian, my co-author of this book, when the call came.

I checked in with Mom when I reached SeaTac airport but she was unable to talk to me. My brother Keith got on the phone but couldn't talk either. Eventually he gave the phone back to Mom, who told me that Dad had passed.

I don't remember what happened after I heard that devastating news. I'm told that I dropped the phone and collapsed.

Ten years before the 9/11 terrorist tragedy it was easier to travel in airports. Somehow, Brian got me on a late flight. My in-laws picked me up at the airport and drove me out to my parents' home at about 3:00 a.m. I crawled up on my mom's bed and held her as we mourned the loss.

I remember taking Mom to the bank the next day to see what money she had. Dad had been in charge of family finances and they were a mess. She came out of the bank and said there was no money. None.

We looked in the strong box where all the important documents were held but there was no life insurance policy there. We couldn't believe it, because early in Dad's career he had sold life insurance.

Mom was 56 years old. Working as a church secretary with no savings, no retirement and a career as a stay-at-home mom, she paid little into Social Security, so the most she could hope for at retirement age was a survivor's benefit.

Mom went through bankruptcy to see that her major bills would be discharged. She was able to stay in the home where she'd been living with Dad thanks to that bankruptcy and she managed very well for herself in the ensuing 20 years.

Recounting this now and remembering how I felt when we learned that Mom had no life insurance or savings, made Dad's loss even greater.

Not only did Mom have no money, but with no life insurance to even bury him and pay for a funeral and burial plot, the rest of the family had to pitch in. It wasn't until years after we buried him that we could afford to add a headstone to mark his grave site. Today, if you went out to pay respects to Dad, you'd be able to find his site because of that headstone.

Don't allow this to happen to you and your family. Insist that the family breadwinners have life insurance and make sure you understand what it's for so you're not caught unaware and unprepared. Also, talk about the family income and savings and if necessary, look into a fixed-index annuity and guaranteed lifetime withdrawal benefit rider.

When life throws you a curve ball, life insurance, and possibly the use of annuities, will help you prepare to hit it. Life insurance and annuities will help you manage your life while helping to financially prepare your family for your eventual death.

PART FOUR: GIVE BETTER

Your financial plan focuses not only on the resources available to you during your lifetime, but also involves what you leave for future generations. We use the term "legacy planning" to encompass both generational transfer and planned charitable giving.

You've worked your entire life to support your family and deserve the peace of mind that a comprehensive estate plan can give you. A good place to start making sure your family receives the maximum benefit from your estate is requesting your free copy of *The Madrona Life and Legacy Planner*. This free-for-the-asking resource is designed to assist you in developing lifetime goals, both personal and financial, and building your legacy so that your loved ones can navigate your estate with clarity once you are unable to do so.

This guide will bring order to your affairs by helping you:

- Consolidate your important documents
- Name who will handle your affairs
- Designate who receives your real estate and valuable items
- Consolidate and provide inventory of your investment accounts
- Express your last wishes

Estate plans need to be designed and executed with a high level of attention to detail in order to minimize related taxes for your family and heirs, allow your assets to pass on outside of probate court and make sure your final wishes are carried out exactly as planned. Even small mistakes can prove to be very expensive and invalidate legal documents.[19]

---

19   Seek counsel from an estate planning attorney.

STEP ON UP

Though I like to step up on the dance floor with my version of the Sprinkler, Churning Butter, and other assorted moves designed to embarrass my wife and kids, that's not what this topic is about. The step up in basis is one of the least understood topics we deal with during our lifetime.

> **WARNING**: *This and many other topics in this book deal with the subject of financial implications after someone passes away. Since statistics show that a vast majority of all mortals will die someday, we shouldn't just bury our head in the sand.*

The subject of Step-Up deals with the situation where you inherit money from your spouse, a family member or a friend.

> **NOTE**: *There are different rules for the deceased who live in a community property state versus a common law state. Those from community property states receive a double-step-up in the case of a spouse. A half-step-up is generally allowed in a common law state.*

As an example of double-step-up in a community property state, meet "Donald" of Washington.

Donald loved to buy a certain kind of rental house. Some would call these fixer uppers, I might call them tear downs! When he passed away, his wife "Betty" was mortified with the prospect of having to own and maintain 20 of these houses, worth about $3 million dollars. The structures had been fully depreciated, so only the cost of the original land remained as basis. This basis was $300,000. Had the houses been sold while they were both alive, there would have been a huge capital gains tax to pay on the gain of $2.7 million.

I suggested she sell them. Betty said she could not sell them because of the tax. So I told her about the step-up in basis and how her new basis was now the fair market value at the date of Donald's death: $3 million. So when she sold the houses, there would be no income tax owed. Her relief was enormous.

Had they lived in a common law state, the result would have been different. Only Donald's half would have received the step-up, not Betty's (hence the term half-step-up). So the new basis would be half of $3 million plus half of $300,000. The taxable gain from the sale after the date of death would therefore be $1.35 million.

Community Property State: Double Step Up
Common Law State: Half Step Up

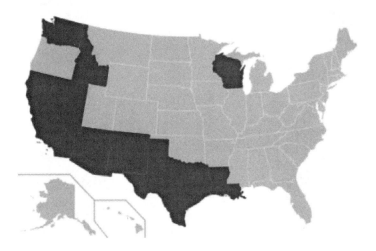

Example: John and Jane Live in California

Cost of Lot	= $100,000
FMV	= $500,000
Gain if gifted or sold	= $400,000
After John or Jane's death, new basis is $500,000 ($300,000 if from Oregon)	

Most assets receive the step-up. Assets that do not get a step up are all IRAs and retirement assets, as well as annuities.

GRANDMA, PLEASE DON'T GIVE ME YOUR HOUSE!

Certain activities such as dentistry, tattooing and estate planning should usually be hired out to someone qualified and not performed at home. Few people know enough to do their own estate planning.

One of my clients consulted with Grandma to gift her real estate during her lifetime in order to avoid probate. There are two major problems with this.

Grandma and Grandpa purchased their residence in Washington State on ten acres in the country, 50 years ago. Grandpa passed away 20 years ago, leaving Grandma with a property valued at $300,000, but today, due to growth in the area, the property is worth $900,000.

If Grandma sells the property during her lifetime, her gain is reduced by $250,000 because it is her residence, so the capital gain is $350,000. Before we go further, let's review that math:

Today's value:	$900,000
Value when Grandpa died	($300,000)
Residence exemption	($250,000)
Capital Gain	$350,000

If Grandma were to pass away and leave the property to her children, they would claim the step-up in basis and pay no tax.

Problem One: A strange thing happens when property is gifted. The original basis goes along with the property. So if the children received the house before Grandma dies and then sell the property, all of the $600,000 gain is taxed, $900,000 less the original $300,000 basis when Grandpa died.

There is no break for it being Grandma's residence and no step-up in basis. This mistake cost the heirs about $100,000 in additional income tax.

Problem Two: Probate may not be that expensive or cumbersome in your state. Avoiding probate may or may not be the best strategy depending on the asset mix and the state of residence. Consult an estate attorney on this question.

How to Ruin Your Grandkids With One Sentence

The most ruinous sentence? Leave them money that is all theirs when they turn 18.

Let's say Grandpa has a fairly sizable estate and knows how hard it is for young people starting out. In his will, he splits $1 million between his five young grandchildren. He doesn't like paying attorneys and doesn't want to burden anyone with trustee duties, so he leaves it to them, certain they have no access to the money until they turn 18. He is quite sure these adorable youngsters will all attend top colleges and will use this money to pay their tuition and maybe have enough left to put a down payment on a house.

Grandson Billy just turned 18. He is a good student and now has two piles of paper in front of him. A pile of college applications and a $200,000 pile of cash. You see, when a minor has a custodial account like an inheritance, they have full access to it all when they turn 18.

Grandpa was quite sure Billy would carefully research his options and make the best decision possible with this inheritance. Billy does carefully weigh his options, and after an exhaustive two-hour research period on his iPad, Billy knows exactly what to do. He buys himself a brand new Tesla and a month-long trip to Vegas for himself and a girl he met last week.

Those college applications have been thrown away. Why would an 18-year-old go to college when he has all that money and a new car?

Granddaughter Sally was a mediocre student, but started hanging out with the wrong crowd. She started dabbling in recreational drugs, but then she received her $200,000. Imagine the parties and high-end drugs she and her so-called friends indulged in for the next six months, the length of time it took to snort through that inheritance. Unfortunately, not only was the money gone, but so was Sally's future.

I will stop there. You get the picture. Could this have been avoided?

Yes. A simple paragraph in your will that provided for the creation of a family trust would have helped greatly here. In my own will, if I die while my kids are still young, the money would be put into trust with my brother as trustee.

From ages 18-24, my brother has been instructed to help them with tuition, room and board, and books. At age 25, my children get a third of what remains. They get half of what remains in trust at age 30, and the final distribution at age 35. This allows them to make a mistake with the first distribution and still retain the opportunity to learn and mature before they receive subsequent distributions.

Raoul, The Pool Boy

Catchy title, but the real topic is "Credit Shelter Trusts: How to Pass Assets to Your Family and Not to Somebody Else's Family."

Here is the situation. You've worked your whole life and you have kids with your wife of many years. You are a pretty smart guy so you do your own simple will and leave everything to your wife, knowing that she will eventually pass everything along to your kids.

Attorneys charge too much anyway, and the $1,000 you just saved will buy you a brand new lawn mower. Brilliant!

What if you pass away prematurely? Remarriages do happen sometimes. Your wife is sitting on a sizable estate and along comes Raoul who sweeps her off her grief-stricken feet. He convinces your wife to allow him to manage the new family estate after they get married. That makes sense, since you used to manage the finances and your wife was never interested in doing so.

Whom do you think will be more likely to end up with your half of the estate and even her half? Your kids? Or Raoul and his kids? My guess is the latter.

With the inclusion of a Credit Shelter Trust (CST) provision in your will, your half of the estate would have gone into a trust. Your spouse would become the beneficiary of the income from the trust, but your children would become the principal beneficiaries.

The purpose of the trust is to provide income, measured as interest, dividend and rental income to be paid to your spouse. The investments are designed to pass estate tax free to the heirs, not to someone unnamed in your will.

> **NOTE**: *The 2015 federal exemption is $5.43 million; the exemption for a married couple is $10.86 million*

Who Gets the Cactus Plant?

I'm not imaginative enough to make the next one up. It really happened.

An elderly mom had three children and all were very close. Indeed, the three sons lived with Mom into their sixties. Yes, the four of them lived together most of their lives, and that's not even the strangest part of this story: one of the boys finally got married and moved out. Shortly thereafter, Mom died leaving one-third of her estate to each of her children.

It was a very simple will since that was Mom's only desire. Simple enough, right?

Fast forward seven years because this estate had not been settled yet. The new wife of one of the sons wanted certain personal effects not discussed in the will. As the years passed, the animosity between these siblings reached absurd levels. After six years of negotiation and threats, they finally got down to splitting up the two remaining assets, Dad's old camera lenses and equipment and a 50-year-old family cactus plant. This almost went to court.

Yes, I did say a cactus plant!

It was at this time the case was assigned to my office. As my own frustration grew with these people, I made the suggestion that with a hammer for the lenses, and a knife for the plant, I could split these up evenly! They weren't awfully impressed with my idea for some reason.

Bottom line here, make sure you identify personal heirlooms in your will, and if you are an executor, make sure personal heirlooms are identified during the person's lifetime to avoid heartburn for yourself after their death. On a related note, make sure you have someone selected to make the final decision for anything not covered in your will.

For example, I was helping my dad write his will. I said to him, "Dad, you have three boys but you have one and only one 1965 cherry red GTO convertible in the barn. Who gets it someday?"

He told me the youngest sibling would get it (darn, I'm the middle kid), so I placed this instruction in his will. I took the additional step to inform my older brother of the decision, and after two days of crying, he came to terms with our dad's decision.

Bottom line, there won't be a fight between us siblings over "stuff" since this and all other family heirlooms are now addressed in my parents' wills.

HAVE YOUR CAKE
AND EAT IT TOO!

You hate paying taxes, but you like helping people, and you have the means to do so. What to do?

Consider my conversation with the Pessimistic Pat.

Me: "Pat, I have a win-win for you."

Pat: "Go on."

Me: "You have that piece of land that only produces a property tax bill for you to pay every six months. You can gift the land to a charitable remainder trust, and get a portion of the gift deducted, based on how old you are. This charitable deduction will get you money back on your taxes until the whole deduction is exhausted. Then you can sell this highly-appreciated asset and pay no capital gains tax on any of the gains because it's now a non-taxable 'charity' selling the land."

Pat: "What else do I get?"

Me: "In addition, the asset is no longer part of your estate, so you can potentially save 40% on estate tax!"

Pat: "Is there anything else?"

Me: "Yes, you can choose a distribution percentage for you and your spouse's joint lives up to about 8% of the annual asset balance."

How is this possible? The tax code allows you to gift highly-appreciated property to a charity and take a tax deduction. The code also allows a charity to sell assets and not pay taxes on gains.

By gifting and therefore giving up control of the asset, it is no longer part of your estate even though you can retain an income benefit for the rest of your lives.

So what is the catch? There is always something, now isn't there? In this case, it is that the remaining principal after the second of you dies goes to the charity of your choice.

Once the trust is established, you no longer have access to the principal and you can never change the beneficiaries from charities back to your children. You can however, during your lifetime, change the charities that will eventually receive the principal.

Here's an example of how the Private Charitable Foundation works with a piece of property that costs $100k with a fair market value of $500,000.

- Receive a charitable deduction
- Pay no tax on $400,000 gain when sold
- No estate tax owed anymore
- Upon second spouse to die, remaining assets go to charity

When Giving Definitely Feels Good!

Giving away your tax liability doesn't feel good, it feels great!

Personally, I serve on several charitable boards for organizations that do phenomenal things in our community. I have found that being a CPA, or a "walking calculator," is a skill that boards of directors need.

As a shameless plug, two of my organizations are the YMCA of Snohomish County, and All God's Children International, which provides care primarily for orphans with disabilities in developing countries, "the least of us."

Whereas board members for corporations get paid, board members for non-profits are expected to donate money to the cause. I always chuckle when someone asks me how much I get paid to sit on these boards, when the reality is that most board members I work with donate thousands of dollars each year, not the other way around. The rewards are not financial; they're much more than can be assigned a dollar value.

Now, imagine giving something besides time and money away, namely your tax liability from your retirement accounts. Under the current tax law, taxpayers are allowed to directly gift money from their retirement accounts to a charity and thereby avoid the tax liability on that distribution.

You might ask why this matters, since donations are already deductible. Can't you just take a distribution from your retirement account and then make an offsetting tax deductible donation?

The answer is that most people 70 years olds and older who don't need all of their retirement money for living expenses already have their houses paid off. This would mean that they may not have enough to itemize their deductions in the first place, making the direct donation produce a higher tax savings.

The charity pays no tax on the retirement money, so if you are so inclined, make this kind of gift and make a difference for someone less fortunate than yourself.

Another way to save on taxes while benefiting a charity is to donate appreciated property or stocks. For example, let's say you own $100,000 of Microsoft that you bought in the mid-1980's. If you sold the stock, you would owe about $15,000 in taxes,[20] with the net of $85,000 going to the charity. Had you gifted the stock directly to the charity, all $100,000 could go to fund its work, with no tax liability and a full $100,000 charitable deduction for you (okay, there are certain limitations outside the scope of this book).

I think you'll agree that saving on income taxes doesn't feel as good as giving to those less fortunate, but it might be a distant second!

---

20   Federal tax, since state and local vary.

MADRONA FINANCIAL SERVICES AT YOUR SERVICE

Madrona Financial Services was founded in 1999 to provide financial expertise that is thorough, transparent and unique, while acting in our clients' best interests as a fiduciary. This fiduciary capacity is not new to our CEO and Chief Investment Officer, Brian Evans, as he has met this standard since beginning his professional career as a CPA more than 30 years ago.

Today, Madrona and our wholly-owned sister company Bauer Evans, Inc. P.S. have grown to include over 30 support staff working together to help you invest in your future, simplify your life and prosper.

This is The Madrona Way and this is why we exist.

At Madrona Financial Services, we pride ourselves on an unparalleled level of client service and appreciate the opportunity to help make your financial ambitions a reality.

Corporate Office | Everett
2911 Bond St Suite 200
Everett, WA 98201
Phone: (425) 212-3777
Phone: 1-844-MADRONA
Email: info@MadronaFinancial.com

BRIAN K. EVANS

Brian is a CPA and Personal Financial Specialist who founded the Madrona Fund ETFs in June 2011. He is primarily responsible for the three funds he manages on the New York Stock Exchange.

He is also principal and owner of Madrona Financial Services, an SEC-registered investment advisory company managing over $100 million of client assets. He is also President and owner of Bauer Evans CPAs, one of the largest certified public accounting firms north of Seattle, serving over 4000 clients.

Brian is nationally published in the Larsten's *The Black Book™ on Personal Finance.* He is also a Guest Analyst on CNBC and Fox Business.

DALE RAYMOND CURTIS

Dale is Madrona Financial Services' branch manager in the Southern California office. He is the Client Relationship Manager and serves on Madrona's Investment Committee while overseeing the marketing and business development efforts.

In his business career, Dale has both founded and sold small business start-ups, and expanded his businesses through the acquisition of other companies.

Dale once led a ministry group that provided leadership and training to over 100 lay-staff volunteers. Today, he serves in his community as a Chaplain.

REQUEST YOUR FREE COPY OF
THE MADRONA LIFE AND LEGACY PLANNER
BY EMAILING
INFO@MADRONAFINANCIAL.COM